# Re-story
# Restore
# Restart

## LEAVE LIMITING
## BELIEFS BEHIND
## AND MOVE FORWARD

*Koralia Timotheou*

# Re think

First published in Great Britain in 2023
by Rethink Press (www.rethinkpress.com)

© Copyright Koralia Timotheou

Cover image © Shutterstock | Elena Shchukina

*To Sophocles, who has a reputation for being wise*

# Contents

# Introduction

This book starts with stories, but what makes stories so important? We create stories just by living. There is a story of how I went to the grocery this morning, how I graduated university, how my start-up company went bankrupt, how my family develops, how I've switched jobs. We each add daily to our personal storyline and to the grand library of human history. We create experience. At the same time, our current reality—how we interpret the present—is affected by our accumulated experience: our personal and collective past stories, what has already happened to and around us.

Subsequently, our individual contemporary stories are added to a huge collective database and become cognitive input for someone else's stories: our children's, our siblings', our friends' and more. To an extent, we all participate in a relay of assumptions, convictions and deductions, stories passing on from one generation to the next, creating common beliefs, thought patterns and world theories. Some of the old stories weaken over time and are overwritten by new, more powerful ones. Others remain alive and influential for many generations. The people who have raised us and those who raised them have lived through circumstances different from ours. We have, therefore, indirectly inherited some of their sensitivities and life views that may no longer be valid or helpful.

In this book, I share stories that have become beliefs and convictions through years of repetition and practice. They have been imprinted on us so deeply we can communicate most of them in just a few words. Stories are stories. What we make out of them is another story. Part One is a collection of fifteen stories that may consistently be misleading us because we interpret them in a certain way. They are deeply rooted in us, and we believe them so blindly that we live by them without question. They shape our reality. Fortunately, it doesn't have to be that way. We can choose not to believe these stories.

While sharing these stories, I am deconstructing and re-storying them. Deconstructing a story means identifying where it comes from and recognizing that it may be subject to alternative interpretations. This doesn't mean we have been wrong all the way. It means it may now be time to change how we read it. When a myth collapses, we strip it of its power to define us and we can leave it behind more easily. A story can then be changed and re-storied. Re-storying is re-telling the story differently. If a story is subject to many interpretations, choosing an empowering version is healthier, more beneficial and more fun than sticking to a disempowering one. It can create a different experience.

While the first part of this book is mostly about *what* (what is the story?), the second and third parts are about *how*. Part Two contains tools that can be used to help release deeply imprinted incapacitating beliefs, long-lived misinterpretations and misconceptions, and lifelong self-destructive habits. This is where we set ourselves free from the grip of unconstructive stories. We restore our forgotten clarity and innocence: how we would have been without those stories misleading us. Most of the tools are based on principles of physics. Life is physics. Philosophers, physicists and other scientists have been pointing this out for thousands of years.[1] It is amazing how skilled we are at ignoring them. Part Three focuses on restarting: redefining how we want life to look and how we want to be in it. It includes more tips, techniques and methods, such as minimalism, decluttering, mindfulness, flow and role play.

This book is constructed around how *I* have re-interpreted stories which are common to many of us. Having experienced the negative impact of stories and associated beliefs in my own life, I have been fortunate enough to find ways round them, with the assistance of my coaches. In turn, I have been blessed with people trusting me to help them disengage from the paralyzing control of disempowering stories and beliefs. My aim is to share my experiences with anyone who wants to break free from limiting convictions, perceive life more simply and clearly, and move toward becoming who they are naturally inclined to be as opposed to who they think they are supposed to be. The book includes ten experiments to help put theory into practice.

If we want to change anything—our health, our finances, the world—we need to shift our thinking by abandoning obsolete and superseded stories, beliefs, thinking patterns and life models, expanding our perception, and creating new stories.

Read on and consume responsibly. We don't have to agree on everything. What applies to one doesn't necessarily suit another. Question, challenge and experiment. Take what works for you and let the rest go.

Be playful.

# PART ONE
## RE-STORYING

Since the beginning of human history, we have been creating stories to explain what we don't yet comprehend.

Once upon a time, Native Americans thought the stars in the sky were the long-gone souls of both humans and animals.[2] The Hindus believed the Earth was supported on the backs of elephants, resting on the back of a turtle.[3] Ancient Greeks were convinced that a bodybuilder by the name of Atlas was holding the Earth on his shoulders.[4] Wonderful stories, but they are just that: stories. As soon as scientific evidence proves them incorrect, stories are deconstructed and re-storied, updated and retold.

This is what we humans do best: make up stories and then invalidate them to generate new ones. We no longer believe it is possible to fall off the edge of the

Earth, but sometimes we are convinced God is punishing us, other people have the power to harm us, we are victims of circumstances, life is a struggle. Two thousand years from now, today's convictions will probably be outdated, even amusing. Until then, these thoughts are our current realities because we believe them. What if most of these realities are nothing more than stories passing from generation to generation? What if none of them is truer than a bolt of lightning being the wrath of gods?

Our stories shape our beliefs; therefore, just as stories can be changed, our beliefs can be questioned and challenged. It doesn't necessarily mean they are wrong. It means:

- Not taking them for granted

- Questioning their applicability

- Testing them

- Using informed, personal decisions to apply them sparingly

- Making choices

- Unlearning what we have assumed for years

At some point in the process, an old dog may choose to learn new tricks and unlearn some of the outdated ones.

It is not hard to re-story a story. A small change in punctuation, interpretation, angle and perspective can turn a story around. Let's rethink some stories!

# 1
# Story 1: The World Is Falling Apart

Is it? Or is this how we perceive it to be?

There is a European folk tale, which goes something like this…[5] Once upon a time, a band of animals lived happily at a poultry farm. One morning, as Chicken Little was plucking worms from the ground, an acorn fell on her head. She didn't know what hit her. The blow was so forceful that she assumed that the sky must be falling. What imminent danger! She had better warn the king. On her way to the palace, she summoned other birds too. Even though they had their reservations, the rooster, the duck, the goose and the turkey joined her in her concern. The party finally came across a fox. The fox volunteered to show them a shortcut to the palace and tricked them into her den, next to a big tree. Fortunately, a couple of the birds were alert. They shook the tree, causing acorns to fall and knock out the fox. The birds managed to escape but not before an acorn fell on Chicken Little's head.

"AHA!" thought Chicken Little. "It was an acorn all along. The sky is not falling after all."

Chicken Little had assumed wrong. She didn't see the acorn when it fell on her head earlier that morning. A simple explanation was there all along, but she couldn't grasp it because she missed an important piece of information. Trying to interpret her experience using her limited perception, she made up a tale of the sky collapsing and the world falling apart. She spread terror to her neighbors, who took her story for granted. When an unfortunate mishap occurs, we let our imagination run wild, jump to conclusions and generalize. A falling acorn is interpreted as the end of the world.

We are bombarded with stories from the media. Some are factual, some are based on assumptions, and others are fabricated. We receive massive doses of information about malice, fear, perversion and manipulation, while examples of kindness, love and compassion rarely make the newscasts. How do we expect to be balanced, healthy and sane when we are exposed daily to such an imbalanced intake of audio-visual material?

Perhaps the world is not falling apart. There are problems to be solved and edges to be rounded, but this doesn't mean the future is bleak. Now, more than ever, we communicate well, accept, respect and help each other. We care.[6] What I read on the internet, hear on the radio or watch on TV is not necessarily representative of how the world is. Selecting reliable news feeds, listening to brief news summaries instead of subjective elaborate analyses, watching informative documentaries and inspiring stories, I balance my exposure to sad and happy news, to distress and hope. Being balanced, I can be helpful and supportive without becoming depleted. Recognizing that there is love, care and beauty in the world makes my efforts seem worthwhile and keeps me motivated and energized.

# 2
# Story 2: I Shouldn't Be Making Mistakes

Thousands of years ago, an ancient civilization invented the wheel. Since then, the wheel has become an asset to humanity and there is no need for each generation to re-invent it. Science advances and society progresses when we capitalize on the expertise of those who came before us.

When I got my first car, I trusted that our ancestors knew what they were doing inventing the wheel. I didn't think it necessary to redesign one. When my dad gave me tried-and-tested driving advice, I refused to listen. A week after I got my license, I decided to take my friends on an excursion to the salt lakes. My dad repeatedly warned me that it wasn't a good idea. It had rained the day before and the lakes would probably be swamped. I was an inexperienced driver and didn't have a four-wheel drive.

Dad asked me: "If you get stuck in there, how will you get out?"

"I won't get stuck," I replied. "I'll only drive on dry ground."

To cut a long story short, we got stuck in the mud. This was the mid-nineties when we had no mobile phones, so we stayed there for hours. Fortunately, another adventurous group showed up. They were experienced and well equipped. They had the proper vehicle and a recovery tow rope with which they pulled us out of the swamp. I went home tired and embarrassed. Why hadn't I listened to my dad? I have no idea.

Whereas in the world of science and technology we eagerly build on each other's findings, we stubbornly insist on making our own mistakes when it comes to learning the ways of life. It is probably in our human nature. We choose to experience life firsthand, to evolve and grow through our personal slip-ups. This is, in a sense, inefficient—I keep repeating common mistakes when I could have avoided them. On the other hand, it allows me to grow at my own pace. This means I can be slow, stuck at the same place for a long time, but also that I have the potential to progress much faster. I can bypass difficulties, overcome obstacles and upgrade more quickly and easily than I thought I could.

If making mistakes is part of our learning process, failure is, to a certain extent, inevitable. What is it, then, that makes us so fearful of it? So unwilling to take risks, embarrassed to make mistakes and reluctant to admit them?

Making mistakes is a social taboo. We make a big deal out of it. One small failure is enough for us to feel that we *are* a failure. We are scared and ashamed. Overcoming my fear to admit my mistakes makes them less painful. It breaks the taboo. When I stop identifying with my failures, they become less important. It is liberating.

Making mistakes is a privilege of those who dare to take action. Sitting on the couch, I can't trip and fall, but do I want to stay on the couch for the rest of my life? Babies fall flat on their faces and hard on their bums all the time when they first start walking. They bruise, they cry, but they don't give up. If they gave up at first failure, our species wouldn't have learned how to walk.

As a mother, I taught myself to say: "I don't know," "I'm not sure," "I was wrong," "I have made a mistake." This was not typical adult behavior when my generation was growing up. I had to practice it until it felt safe and natural. I made the effort because I didn't want my children to grow up thinking they are supposed to be perfect at everything. I didn't want them to be scared or embarrassed of being wrong and ashamed of making mistakes.

Instead of seeking perfection, it is more practical to embrace our imperfections and work *with* them rather than *against* them. To this end, it is important to establish safety in making mistakes. This can improve our learning experience, personal development and well-being. Safety comes with ownership. Making mistakes is easy. Denying them is a piece of cake. Owning them is not. Owning up to my mistakes allows me to benefit from them and move on.

# 3

# Story 3: Time Heals And I Will Survive

In my late thirties, I burned out. "Just hang in there," people would say. "Switch to survival mode until the storm is over." "Give it time and things will sort out by themselves." And so I did.

This was the worst piece of advice I ever applied. The storm was not outside. It was inside me and it was only getting worse. Without my purposeful intervention, time alone wouldn't sort anything out. My problems wouldn't just go away on their own. Where was I expecting them to go, anyway? They hadn't appeared by themselves in the first place. *I* had created them, so *I* had to undo them. It was up to me to figure out how.

As time went by and I did nothing to address the problem, my body reacted in an effort to escape from a situation that was becoming unbearable. Since I did not seem willing to act decisively, my body took action *for* me. Up to then, I had been a healthy person, but at that point my body started malfunctioning in many ways. Physicians couldn't identify the source of the problem and the symptoms were getting worse. It finally became clear to me that my body was expressing its deep dissatisfaction in an effort to get my attention, forcing me to take action. Alarmed, I realized the downfall wouldn't stop unless I did something about it.

This is how I learned that time alone isn't always enough. Time could only give me time. It was up to me to use that time wisely to reboot and restart. It was hard, but in retrospect I can appreciate what a blessing this was. If all my problems could be solved by time alone, I wouldn't have broken free from overwhelming situations, and unhealthy behaviors and thinking patterns. I would have gone on existing, from birth to death, without discovering and unfolding myself.

I also recognized that survival mode wasn't working for me. I could do better. I could do differently. In its wisdom, my body would go on complaining for as long as it had to. It would only stop when I stopped operating in a state of scarcity and when I had better goals than just getting through the day. My health was deteriorating simply because there was no stimulation, excitement or inspiration where I was; no momentum or purpose. There was just breathing, eating, sleeping and working. It wasn't enough. My inner self wasn't interested in surviving. She wanted to thrive.

We are made to evolve, to continuously upgrade and progress. If this weren't the case, we would still be living in caves. We are wired to thrive in whatever appeals to us, in what we do best—in being a surgeon, a teacher, a hairdresser; in raising a family, a garden, farm animals; in making art, music, cookies. In anything. *This* is the beauty of diversity.

Life is my opportunity to experience the material world and express myself through my physical form: my body. What am I offering? What am I receiving? Am I sharing with the world or am I hiding from people? Do I keep waiting for something big to happen? How about making it happen right now? Is it ever going to be the right time to make a move? How about making that move today? Am I waiting for better days? What is keeping me from having a beautiful day every day?

It is true that we can live on just bread and water; but is this what we want? We are restless by nature. We are explorers and achievers. We have creative minds and eager souls. As soon as we detect potential, we want to go for it. Unlike all other known species, we operate on multiple levels, consecutively and in parallel. Succeeding in one level leads to temporary satisfaction and short term happiness, but this feeling of contentment doesn't last long. It is soon replaced by an appetite for more.

# Operating consecutively

According to Maslow's hierarchy of needs and human motivation theory,[7] there are five consecutive levels of human evolution:

1. **Level One:** Thousands of years ago, humankind was striving to fulfill its biological needs: food, water, shelter, clothing, sex and sleep. Once basic needs were met, we were satisfied for a while. Before long, we wanted more.

2. **Level Two:** We sought safety, security, predictability and control. We expanded our families and developed communities. We came up with specializations and professions: we became hunters, builders, farmers, doctors and teachers. We made group arrangements and acted as leaders, legislators, arbitrators. We set rules for the protection of life and property.

3. **Level Three:** It is no surprise that, when levels one and two had been achieved, we moved toward the fulfillment of more intangible needs. We yearned for a sense of belonging. We wanted to socialize, connect, communicate, convey, collaborate, contribute, complete each other: all the beautiful "co" concepts; the things we do together; those that take more than one of us. We invested in love, friendship, companionship, sharing and volunteering. We created social structures: marriage, family, professional bodies,

sports clubs and political parties. Of course, at that point, we also started to control, command, conspire, corrupt, condemn. These are the cons, the downside of "cos," but that's another story.

4. **Level Four:** Soon, participating in these social structures was no longer enough. We longed to be acknowledged, heard, appreciated, respected and admired. We wanted to stand out. We craved status, rank, prestige, recognition, credit and authority.

5. **Level Five:** When the applause dies away, we turn inward. The glamour of social life doesn't look as attractive as it used to. Peace of mind, serenity, love and generosity feel more important. Admiration and ovation from the audience are not a requirement anymore. This performance is for one spectator only.

The concept of progress from one level to the next applies to humanity as a group and to each person individually. We are not all in sync. During the Stone Age, when most people were striving to survive, humanity as a whole was at level one, while a handful of individuals were already at level five. Currently, more people are at levels two, three and four than at level one. We have progressed as a group, but none of the levels have disappeared. All five co-exist. We therefore need to be patient with each other. Maslow's model helps us comprehend human behavior and the reason we don't all want the same things. It also explains our thirst for more. Surviving is not enough. Wanting more is innate to our species. We are born to thrive.

## Operating in parallel

Many of us succeed in some aspects of life but feel we are failing in others. Career, family, romance, finance, friendship and social interaction are facets of life that run in parallel. It is easy to be accomplished in one but feel lacking in another. As a result, we are miserable even when we thrive in all but one. We want it all, don't we?

# 4
# Story 4: I Am A Victim

For twenty years, I worked in the corporate world, both as an employee and as a freelancer. I've had wonderful working and learning experiences. Along with these, some frightening, upsetting and disappointing incidents have occurred.

I was at a client's premises, working alongside one of their senior managers when I felt a hand touching my knee under the conference table. Assuming it must have been involuntary, I didn't immediately react. The hand stayed where it was and could no longer be mistaken for an accident. I shook it off and stood up. Turning to the hand's owner for an explanation, I was faced with an inappropriate suggestion. I darted out of the room, into the corridor and straight to my car, crying my way back home. It took me days to shake off the sensation of that uninvited touch. I never returned to that client and the incident ended there. I didn't tell anyone. I didn't even find the courage to ask for the fees for my work.

Fifteen years later, I was giving a presentation for a client. The meeting room was full of people of all ages and genders. As soon as I paused to take questions, one of the male participants turned to me and made a rude and unprofessional innuendo. I glanced around in disbelief at the people in the room. No reaction. I must have heard wrongly. The guy repeated his comment. I looked at him and replied coldly that since this was a professional meeting, I would take a note to discuss his comments with the project management team and get back to him. The next morning, I received a phone call. A certain lawyer wanted to clarify a possible misunderstanding between myself and her client during the previous day's meeting. She also wanted to know whether I would pursue any legal action. I said that I would think about it and left both her and her client hanging in uncertainty. I completed the project on schedule with no problems. My fees were paid on time as agreed and no one ever bothered me again.

I was lucky. Not all stories have happy endings. Many are a lot worse than mine. I don't wish to compare my stories to anyone else's; I want to compare my own two stories with each other. What these two real-life stories had in common was *me*. What was different in each case was also me. The first time, I was taken aback. I felt threatened, disoriented and I automatically switched into fight or flight mode: I fled and I didn't stand up for myself. I gave up the client, the project and the fees because I couldn't deal with what had happened. I felt victimized, helpless, embarrassed and exposed. I became reactive. The second time, I knew better. I maintained my composure and neutralized the threat.

Sadly, it isn't always feasible to turn a story around by 180 degrees, but this is an example of how similar events can trigger different responses from the same person if perceived and handled differently. Accepting that I don't control other people's behavior, at least I can choose mine to the degree that feels possible in each situation. It is not always easy, but it is worth giving it a shot because it's all I can do to protect myself from becoming someone's victim.

I increasingly realize how widespread and damaging our victim perspective is. We may indeed be victims occasionally, but feeling victimized all the time is no longer an experience; it becomes a state of mind, a habit. Feeling victimized for something trivial is not only damaging to us, but is an insult to people who have suffered raw violence: physical, emotional or verbal.

What makes us fall so easily back into playing the victim?

It is easier to perceive ourselves as victims than to face failure. It is more comforting to believe that someone else is responsible for our misery than to admit our weakness. We eagerly declare ourselves victims of the system, the government, the politicians, corruption, the society, a war, a pandemic. There is always something or someone out of our control. There always will be. No matter what we do, external circumstances, uncontrolled parameters, powerful people, conflicting interests, hidden agendas, viruses, bacteria, natural and human-made disasters will exist. It is tempting to dump all responsibility onto them.

In doing so, we are sticking our heads in the sand, disempowering ourselves. The government, the society and any social structure are systems that we—people—create. They are *our* constructs and they bear our most dominant group characteristics. If the system is corrupted, the government manipulative, society cruel, it is because we make it or allow it to be so. Blaming any human-made system is a fallacy.

Acting the victim becomes an excuse for me to give up and justify my procrastination, mistakes and failures. This attitude can poison my life by allowing resentment and hopelessness to pile up and paralyze me. Feeling victimized and believing life is unfair can hold me hostage in a vicious circle of disappointment and withdrawal. I gradually give up on life.

Leaving aside extreme situations of mistreatment, victimization—as an ongoing emotion—makes us prone to blaming. When *I* am the victim, there is someone else to blame. It is not *my* fault so it must be someone else's. Our eagerness to accuse each other of all sorts of things is impressive. What we often fail to grasp is that, in addition to potentially harming the accused, blaming hurts the accuser. Even though attributing blame elsewhere may feel like a relief in the short term, in the long term it breeds helplessness and piles up anger and bitterness. Helplessness is incapacitating as it limits possibility. Anger and bitterness are self-destructive and unhealthy.

For everything that happens to me, I consciously or unconsciously give my consent. Our consent being required is an evolutionary gift of our species. This is sometimes hard to accept, but it is important that I do. I consent consciously when I decide to do something in full awareness of the consequences. When I pull an all-nighter, I know I will feel exhausted and disoriented for the next couple of days. I walk around like a zombie, but this is what I have chosen.

Sometimes I consent to something without realizing it. When I desperately wish for a relationship but keep attracting the wrong people and end up getting hurt, I am neither unlucky nor a victim of manipulative individuals. I unconsciously allow this to happen because I have wounds to heal and thinking patterns to overcome. I am not yet ready to move on. I still have one more iteration to go, one more failure to endure, until I arrive at the AHA! that will shift my behavior and change my life.

Not being a victim means I am not a scapegoat. I don't assume responsibility for problems I haven't created unless I specifically choose to. If I occasionally make a choice to bear someone else's responsibility, it is because I feel strong and confident and want to help them, not so they can unload their responsibilities onto me. When I am covering for someone, I ask myself this question: "Am I willingly helping here or am I being cornered?" Only I know the answer.

I recognize I am acting like a victim when I feel or speak in a manner that gives away helplessness. It usually sounds like this:

- They are ripping off taxpayers (they = the government).

- They are manipulating us (they = the politicians).

- They neglect me (they = my parents, friends, family, colleagues).

- I have given up everything for you (you = my spouse or partner).

- I have made so many sacrifices for them (them = my children).

Is it really about them, or am I making lousy choices and allowing people to walk all over me?

Taking ownership and responsibility means thinking differently, re-storying the thoughts above in a more empowered way:

- I am paying high taxes, but I am grateful that I do. It means I am one of the lucky people who make a lot of money.

- It looks like politicians are lying, but I don't have to buy into it. I vote, I speak, I take initiatives. I can make a difference, no matter how small.

- I didn't get the attention and care I wanted from my parents as a child, but because of that, I now know how to parent my own children differently. I also know how to take care of myself.

- I quit my job because I wanted to move in with you, but it seems we don't have the same priorities. This is fine because it was *my* decision, which I can now change any time I want to.

- I wanted to be a devoted mother and raise my children. Putting my career on hold was a good option at the time. I don't regret it. Now it is time to resume my work.

How I dialogue with my mind shapes how I feel about myself and life.

# 5
# Story 5: You Have A Problem? Don't Think About It

When I was a little girl, my parents went on a week-long trip abroad and my grandparents came to stay with me. I set up camp in my father's study, squeezing my textbooks between chunky computers, printers and fax machines, pretending to be boss while attempting my homework. Unfortunately, I left a glass of my favorite smoothie on my dad's wooden desk for the entire week. When I decided to tidy up on the day of my parents' return, I was horrified to see a clearly visible round stain on the old oak desk. Running out of time and options, I rearranged the printer so that it covered the stain. Then I forgot about it.

Weeks later, my dad summoned me to his study. He was furious at me, and I couldn't understand why. It turned out he had found the stain. He was twice as angry with me, first for causing the damage and then for trying to conceal it. What made things worse was that I did not anticipate any of this as I had put the incident behind me. I was caught by surprise. What did I expect? The stain was there and all I had done was hide it, pretending that hiding it was enough to make it disappear. Of course, it wasn't. Where would the stain have gone? It was still there a month later and I got punished twice as hard. Not thinking about something may be putting it to sleep, but it doesn't make it disappear.

When I am fearful, I may prefer not to think about it, but it's better to deal with the problem and resolve it instead of it haunting me in the middle of a future crisis. Thinking about something doesn't mean over-thinking it; it means being aware of its presence, finding its root cause and letting it go. Ruminating over a hurtful situation, recreating and reliving it over and over is equally as damaging as pretending a fearful emotion is not there when it is. Shoving stuff under the carpet doesn't work. I am bound to come across it at some point later, and by then it may have accumulated a lot of grime. If *I* don't clean under my carpet, who will?

# 6

# Story 6: Resist Temptation. Enjoyment Is Sin

We have demonized pleasure so much that we have forgotten how to enjoy what is naturally beautiful and beneficial. We deprive ourselves of innocent joys. There is nothing wrong with enjoying life—far from it. If we didn't have the good times, what would make enduring the hard times worthwhile?

If we are interested in thriving, enjoyment is not a luxury. The point isn't to have a hectic day so as to enjoy ourselves for half an hour. Isn't it better to enjoy the day in its entirety as much as possible on a day-to-day basis? Enjoyment is necessary to relax, reboot, re-energize and rebalance; it shields us when things get rough. When I feel depleted, sad or anxious,

I focus on the little luxuries that give me joy. Sipping a cup of coffee, watching the rain out of my window or taking a bubble bath with lavender essential oils and Epsom salts.

Temptation is overrated. When I feel tempted to do something I supposedly shouldn't, instead of beating myself up, I can use this awareness to gain valuable information about myself. It signifies that I have an unmet need worth investigating. What is amiss here? What is the underlying unmet need? Can I meet it in a safe and sustainable way without harming anyone (including myself)? Indulging in food sometimes reveals a lack of safety and affection. This is the reason we call sweets and snacks "comfort food." When I am lurking around the ice-cream bucket, what I really need is a hug. The point is not resisting the ice cream but getting the hug. Of course, it's fine to eat a bowl of ice cream, but it is even better to get the love and care I am craving. In doing so, I will no longer need the ice cream so fervently and I can enjoy it in reasonable quantities.

Resisting life's little pleasures doesn't help. It renders me a living resistor. In physics, the current running through a circuit of a given voltage is inversely proportional to the resistance(s) of the circuit. According to Ohm's Law,[8]

$$I = V/R$$

where $I$ = the circuit's current measured in amperes (A), $V$ = the voltage, measured in volts (V), and $R$ = the resistance, measured in ohms ($\Omega$)

I compare voltage with life's available driving force pushing the flow of my life's current. It's my qi. The higher the resistance, the lower my current. The more I resist life, the more stuck I get and the fewer things I enjoy. My life is not in flow. I need to do more pushing to get by.

Consistently shutting out life's pleasures piles up deprivation, regret, self-resentment, victimization and anger. It enhances feelings of scarcity and inadequacy. It keeps me unsatisfied. I don't need to indulge in expensive, extravagant or damaging habits to be satisfied. The best things in life are simple, easy and free. Joy is found in simplicity.

# 7
# Story 7: Guilt Makes Me A Better Person

Guilt is the uneasy feeling I have done something wrong that I now regret and blame myself for. It's a dense, unproductive emotion that paralyzes me. It is a self-judging, tormenting situation, destructive to my health and my life. Holding on to it, I enter a never-ending mistake-guilt-blame cycle that serves no one. I feel embarrassed and numb, and find it difficult to make amends to the people I have hurt or to forgive myself. Judging myself, I become judgmental of others. To quit blaming people, I first need to stop blaming myself. I can appease guilt by owning my mistakes, admitting to them, genuinely apologizing and cultivating self-love.

I sometimes feel guilty not for doing something, but for feeling happy. We are taught that feeling good is scandalous when the rest of the world is suffering.

Political and religious leaders often use guilt to control people by invoking fear and shame. They remind us:

- If you are too happy, you are pushing your luck. It will backfire.

- If you stretch yourself too far, you will fall.

- If you seek too much, you will be punished.

- If you laugh a lot, you will regret it.

To be functional I need to feel good, and this requires filling my cup first. For twenty years, family has been my priority, but when I neglect myself too much, I have no energy or strength to support and care for them. When I keep myself healthy and happy, I have more to offer, and I am in a better mood while doing it. Taking time to relax by getting a massage, having my hair done, taking a walk by myself, reading my book by the fireplace, going for a coffee with my friends or staying in bed a little longer in the morning are ways I reboot. I used to feel guilty enjoying myself while my to-do list was growing longer, but being alive and healthy means there *will* be long lists of things to do. If I wait to finish them before I can start enjoying life, I will keep waiting forever.

While guilt is unnecessarily destructive when allowed to linger, it can be beneficial if kept short and sweet. It is the trigger for mentally going back to identify my mistakes and correct them or prevent their re-occurrence. Once it has served this purpose, guilt's job is over. This is easier said than done. We may ponder our blunders all day, but then go and repeat them or do nothing to make amends. *Knowing* what we have done wrong is not enough. We need to *apply* the lesson learned and let the guilt go.

When I look back into my personal history, I find destructive, repetitive patterns of behavior. This signifies there are lessons I haven't yet mastered. Perhaps I am habitually attracting needy people into my life, or I am too open with others and they try to take advantage of me. Maybe I give away a lot of energy and run out of fuel. Identifying patterns in others is easier than identifying them in my own life; I am too close and too involved to detect them. If I take a step back and observe myself from some distance, it is doable.

Detecting patterns, identifying root causes and healing wounds, I am capitalizing on my experiences. Next time something similar happens, I can apply what I have learned and get a different result. If I use guilt to guide me in the right direction and subsequently release it, I have the opportunity to mend, upgrade and advance. As long as I know where to draw the line, my weaknesses can become my strengths and my mistakes can lead to successes. If I recreate and re-experience the past without actively healing, accepting the learning points or strengthening myself, I end up with the opposite results. I identify so deeply with my mistakes, patterns and downfalls that, instead of releasing them, I become more attached to them. Repeatedly rehearsing my past failures, I risk becoming addicted to pain and self-destruction. This makes it more difficult to escape. To get out of the pattern, I need to *intentionally* disturb it. It won't happen on its own.

# 8

# Story 8: I Need To Suppress The Ego

The word "egotism" is used to describe self-centered and selfish behavior. It is an inhibitor to generosity and kindness. We are called to fight, tame or suppress our ego and control our impulses. Fighting the ego, instinct and desire entails resistance, conflict, struggle, loss of energy and exhaustion. Perhaps, instead of fighting or suppressing, it is possible to guide the ego and gently lead it in the right direction.

When I act selfishly or egotistically, it is not because I am an inherently bad person; I am probably missing the big picture. I am disconnected from the world and don't comprehend my place in it. As a result, I am insecure and fearful. I become aggressive, controlling and oppressive because I feel threatened. I am willing to do anything to ensure my survival. I gather possessions, money, praise and power without giving anything away, worrying: "What if I run out of them? What if they are taken away from me?"

I don't want to fight or suppress the ego, but I would be naive to ignore it. I can make the ego porous, or I can make it an ally. The ego becomes as porous as a sieve when I allow occurrences to come through without holding any residual resentment. I didn't get it my way. So what? Does it really matter? Ego becomes my ally when I align my personal desires with the interests of the larger group, the community, the society. My impulses no longer exclusively serve myself. By re-establishing my place in the world, reconnecting with people and nature, learning how reality manifests and what fundamentally matters, the ego is reassured and can find its way home. No struggle is required. Like a pampered pet, the ego wants to be satisfied, loved and informed. In these circumstances, it naturally co-operates. All I need to do is take it by the hand and guide it to the place where the beliefs "not everything is about me" and "it is all about me" coincide.

# 9

# Story 9: I Have Great Expectations

We all have expectations but focusing on them too much gets in the way of sustaining healthy and happy relationships and enjoying life.

As a young mother, even though I was raising three wonderful children, the frequency at which I pointed out their shortcomings was much higher than the frequency at which I complimented them or praised their achievements. I considered it my duty to indicate their flaws to help them improve. I scolded them for being late, for forgetting, for doing and for not doing. I hardly ever congratulated them for making their bed, for washing the dishes, for studying without complaining. My behavior wasn't balanced. I loved them, but it wasn't always obvious; it often seemed like I was staring at the one and only stain on an otherwise spotless window. I expected my children to be impeccable, but instead of encouraging them by acknowledging their accomplishments, I discouraged them by consistently pointing out where they fell short.

I have three kinds of expectations: what I expect of life, others and myself. Having specific expectations of life is a recipe for disappointment. Things don't always turn out as planned. With my life mapped out to its finest details, I am bound to encounter deviations and to face struggles and frustration. Being fixated on preconceived results limits the possible outcomes and reduces the probability of something better showing up.

Expecting less, I experience fewer disappointments and am more pleased when things turn out favorably. Keeping plans to a minimum and focusing more on the *direction* than the interim results is healthier. What may look like a failure, a setback or an obstacle may later prove to be a blessing, an opportunity, an opening. Instead of wasting my energy worrying and complaining every time things don't work out exactly as I expect them, I can remain open to any benefits that come my way, keeping in mind that all I need is to be healthy and happy—nothing more, nothing less.

My expectations of others depend on how I see myself expressed through them and how needy I am in a relationship. My children are—to an extent—a reflection of me; it may be that my partner and some of my closest friends are, too. Pushing my children to succeed, do well or accomplish something could be mistaken for love, when it is driven by my need to seek credit through *their* achievements. If I want them to do well for themselves, I support them, but I don't *push* them. I don't project my own needs, insecurities and aspirations onto them. They have their own. I don't expect them to succeed to satisfy *me*. I prefer them to cultivate self-respect, self-love and self-care for their own sake. Expecting too much of them suffocates them. They may underperform and feel miserable.

Perceiving myself reflected in a loved one's behavior also causes friction and disappointment. I forget that people are who they are regardless of what they are *to me* and I get upset because I'd rather they had acted differently. When this happens, I remind myself they are independent individuals, and they will not always act according to my values. Detaching myself from their decisions, behavior and course of action helps me love them more genuinely. Distinguishing myself from them in my mind, I don't get reactive about everything they say or do. I am more comfortable and relaxed with them and we can co-exist more happily. I am not responsible for them and they are not responsible for me either.

The expectations I have of myself are my strongest motivators in life. I set goals based on those expectations and work toward them. Achieving these goals is a significant determinant of how I feel about myself. I don't need to lower my standards to feel accomplished. What I want to do is focus on the person I want to be, rather than on specific achievements. This way, no matter what happens, I can keep working toward an increasingly peaceful, confident and loving self, finding reasons to be happy and celebrate life.

# 10

# Story 10: Our Motives Are Complicated

De-composing stories and seeking the source of my behavior, I find that what drives my actions boils down to one of two huge forces: love and fear. Even when it seems that something else is dictating my actions, by peeling off the layers I arrive at one of these two emotions.

This clarity helps me realize that when I am aggressive, offensive or hurtful the reason is *me* and how *I* feel in a person's presence or under certain circumstances. Whenever I behave poorly, I consider what my feelings were shortly *before* showing my ugly face. Perhaps my fears have woken up; my insecurities have come to the surface; I may have been reminded of my shortcomings. Maybe something has put me on edge and I'm now in defense. Perhaps I am tired or in pain: when my stamina is reduced, my fight or flight mechanism kicks in. Knowing how this works, I can consciously relax, realign myself and make amends. I can also explain how other people behave toward me. Their behavior is rarely about me. It is about *them*, so I don't have to take it personally.

Fear is often well disguised and shows up as hostility, anger, resentment, grief, confusion, victimization, rejection, helplessness and hopelessness. It may not be easy to detect at first. Getting to the root cause requires intention and persistence. Low emotions, destructive behavior, violence and rudeness arise from insecurity. Fear brings out the worst in us.

We've been raised to fear:

- Failure—in exams, jobs, ventures, relationships

- The loss of health, loved ones, money, possessions, social status, serenity

- Being exposed as imperfect, weak, soft, vulnerable, incompetent

- Being misunderstood, rejected, abandoned, unloved, unforgiven

- That which is and those who are different

- What we don't understand

- The unpredictable

- Change

Fear's job is to protect us from imminent danger; for example, when crossing a busy road, walking alone at night in certain parts of the city, approaching the edge of a cliff, suddenly hearing a detonation. If we allow it to, it does more than that. It infiltrates our everyday life, our actions and decisions. We become suspicious and see foes everywhere. We are all afraid of something, but when we are scared of a lot of things, our reality becomes a frightening experience. This can be disempowering. Fear is powerful. It paralyzes us, wears us down and drains life out of us. It even causes disease. It prevents us from trying things out, enjoying ourselves and having fun. It deprives us of our happiness. In today's world, we have fewer threats, but we experience more fears.

The opposite of fear is love. When I am afraid, I don't have the energy to love. When I love, I am fearless. What I fear, I want to destroy. When I love, I create. We are creator beings; we create all the time. Love is our natural state of being. It is the antidote to fear. My fears subside when I focus on and magnify the emotion of love.

Being fearless doesn't mean that nothing harmful can ever happen to me. It means I lovingly and proactively tend to my needs without fearing the worst-case scenario. I am more effective when I aim to remain healthy as part of an overall self-care, self-love routine than when I strive to avoid illness. Fearing for my health can be counterproductive. Focusing on what I don't want to happen may materialize the fearful scenario. Lovingly concentrating on my wellbeing is more likely to lead to the desired effect. Praying to avoid illness is not as effective as praying to be healthy. If I am going to direct my mind and energy to something, it might as well be the positive version. I have screwed up job interviews because I was afraid of messing them up. I can now see how my fear of rejection made me look incompetent and resulted in… rejection. Dreading a scenario doesn't scare it away. Concentrating on it magnifies it and avoiding it becomes harder.

When my children were younger, I needed to be in control of their lives. I wanted to ensure they dressed warmly, ate well, slept, exercised, studied and had healthy relationships with their friends. I did that because I loved them but also because I was scared. I feared they would get cold or ill, be rejected or feel disappointed. I was terrified they would suffer. Overwhelming them with advice, being overprotective, scolding them for nonsense and pointing out their mistakes were signs of *my* fear. Then I realized that by being anxious, I was raising stressed children instead of happy ones. This realization helped me change. As I am now driven more by love and less by fear, I am more relaxed in my approach. I am sending out empowering, loving and confident energy instead of nervous and fearful vibes. Kids intuitively know this. My children sense it in my tone of voice, my choice of words and my gestures, and they are more receptive. Children are generally empathic and sensitive to their parents' stress and fear. It scares them to have a scared parent. Instead of transmitting my fear to them, I now operate from a place of love and trust. Confidence, ownership and courage are contagious from parent to child.

Love starts from within. Self-love is a prerequisite for loving others. A wolf who feels safe and content and has a full stomach is unlikely to attack. A lioness who senses her cubs are threatened is guaranteed to be aggressive. A famished tiger will definitely strike because her survival is at stake. We are no different. Fear drives our hostility, while love and self-contentment make us friendly and co-operative. Acknowledging that it is either love or fear that shapes my behavior, my beliefs, thoughts and, ultimately, my reality, I can make conscious choices about the quality of fuel that runs my life's engine: my energy.

# 11

# Story 11: I Know Exactly Who I Am

I am officially a mongrel. Some years ago, I took a DNA ethnicity test. Not surprisingly, it revealed that I am an interesting amalgam of seven distinct ethnicities: 38% Greek, 17% West Asian, 12% North African, 11% Iranian, 11% Middle Eastern, 6% Italian and 5% Ashkenazi Jewish. Knowing this, I feel at home everywhere.

We assume an identity and attach to it. Consequently, we are tied for life to a particular way of living or a significant personality trait: I am an engineer; I am loud and overwhelming; I am shy; I am an introvert; I am vegetarian. What if I change my mind? What if I don't want to always be that? I am a mother. Is that all? I am tired. I am lazy. I am lost. Can't I change who I am? Attaching to a specific identity, I find myself bound to a long-term contract.

The energy required to stick to it when everything around is changing is tremendous and unnecessarily exhausting. Resembling the plastic ID card I carry in my purse, an identity is inflexible and brittle. I can't easily bend it without breaking it. Adopting lifelong identities can be restrictive because I, consciously or subconsciously, identify with them and what they supposedly represent, whereas there is a lot more to me as a person. Hiding behind my identity can also be an excuse for not attempting things that, deep down, I want to do.

Instead of sticking to an identity, I prefer taking on roles. A role is more flexible and doesn't consume me 24/7. I don't feel obliged to identify with it fully and continuously. A role is a light, temporary agreement. I can go in and out of it as I please. Switching roles doesn't make me unreliable. On the contrary, when I voluntarily choose my roles, I am more motivated, willing and energized, and I perform them better.

Adopting a variety of roles is more like working on several projects in parallel than signing up for a permanent full-time job. I can take up more than one role and satisfy more parts of my multilateral personality. I can be a professional, a wife, a mother, a woman, a friend, a daughter, an artist, a citizen, a sports fan, a traveler and an explorer, all in the same week. I can be serious and silly, spontaneous and reserved, serene and excited on the same day. Even though I don't always *seem* to be consistent, this is who I am: the inconsistent me. As I change over time, my needs and priorities change. It's a relief to know I can re-adjust my life roles accordingly.

Sometimes I, too, fall into the trap of assuming I can predict the reactions, behavior and responses of others. When they surprise me, I remind myself it's not *they* who are unpredictable; it is *I* who has assumed I can safely make predictions. They have multiple roles, too. The bank teller who frustrates me by taking his time for every transaction is also an employee with a boss looking over his shoulder. I wish he were quicker, but to him, it is probably more important to keep clear of mistakes. The rude cab driver is also a concerned daughter. She may be edgy because her father is in the hospital for surgery today. My child's impatient schoolteacher is also a wife who may be having a hard time at home. I neither need nor want to justify every behavior, but I can appreciate there is cause for it. We are professionals, parents, mates, friends and much more. Having trouble with one of our roles may affect other roles. It is not always easy to switch from one role to the other.

# 12

# Story 12: I Am Entitled To Happiness

Over the years, I have observed that my satisfaction in life is not always proportional to the
magnitude of my success. My sense of achievement
is often relative to the *effort* and not the *result*. This is
because I then feel I deserve it. Sometimes, even getting something marginally done is sufficient, and I am
content and happy. At other times, no matter what I
do, it never seems enough. This happens when I feel
entitled.

Entitlement is the belief that the world owes me.
Life owes me justice, opportunities, a chance, happiness. It is my turn to shine, to succeed, to make
money. Believing I am entitled to something doesn't
necessarily mean I feel I deserve it as a person. Instead
of feeling worthy of happiness, I believe happiness should be given to me because so many others

already have it or because I have been waiting for it long enough. Entitlement is a limiting emotion. When I feel entitled, I become impatient and frustrated if I don't immediately get what I expect. Entitlement may lead to unrealistic expectations and disappointments. Feeling entitled yet unsatisfied makes me think I am doing something wrong. I am supposed to be happy. Why aren't I?

Gratitude is the feeling of deep thankfulness. It is a heartfelt, happy, peaceful emotion that makes me instinctively want to smile. It results from feeling deserving, that I am worthy of success and happiness. I feel pride in myself, appreciation for all those who have helped me and am grateful to the Universe for its abundance. Experiencing gratitude is the best prayer of acknowledgment. It helps my heart open and expand. It is the antidote to entitlement.

When I don't feel gratitude for the blessings in my life, I probably need to work on my self-worth. Worthiness is often associated with hard work, but not always. Sometimes a smart or proactive move or just good luck beats long working hours. This doesn't make my worthiness any less because there is a reason for what happens. When I get lucky, it is not a random occurrence. It is the Universe having my back and taking good care of me while I am being the best version of myself every day. I give love to the world, and it pays off. I receive everything I need. We all have the right to be happy, but it is difficult to relax and enjoy ourselves when we feel entitled. When we feel worthy, we can appreciate life more. Happiness is not a reward or a trophy. We are heirs to happiness because we are loved. Gratitude and entitlement are choices. It is all about *how* I choose to perceive everything I have. When striving to survive, I want life to be fair, to give me what I believe I am entitled to. I feel entitled to electricity, hot water and a car because so many people have them. When I am in a thriving mindset, everything becomes a gift. I feel gratitude for the simplest things because they make my life easier and more enjoyable.

Gratitude brings people together. Through it we acknowledge how we have benefited from others. I am grateful to our ancestors for inventing the wheel, to Thomas Edison for an effective light bulb,[9] to Orville and Wilbur Wright[10] for those first flights and to my neighbor for that bag of juicy grapefruit. I am glad these people existed and shared their gifts, generosity and enthusiasm with the world and with me. Thinking of them, I send loving, thankful thoughts.

Through gratitude, we can feel rich, proud and accomplished as humanity. Through entitlement, we mostly feel the lack of what we still expect to happen.

# 13

# Story 13: What Doesn't Kill Me Makes Me Stronger

When I was a little girl, my parents thought I was too sensitive—which I was. I often came home from school crying over conflicts among other children. It didn't matter that I wasn't directly involved; I was overwhelmed because I was picking up on the other children's emotional states. My parents tried to toughen me up. More than three decades later, I am no tougher. I am still emotional and sensitive to other people's feelings and lingering energies.

I *have* changed, but instead of becoming tougher, I am coming to terms with my sensitivities. I now know where they come from and how they play out. I am learning to take care of myself, especially when things get rough. When I need to cry, I cry. When I want to laugh, I laugh. I don't hold back emotions when they are seeking a way out. If I do, they will pile up and things will get worse.

What doesn't kill me makes me stronger. How?

- By raising barriers, walls and fences around me?

- By teaching me to pretend not to care, when I do?

- By leading me to adopt other people's reactions, even though they don't resonate with me?

- By forcing me to switch to an endless survival mode?

- By making my heart hard as stone?

- By resulting in me trying to be someone I am not—indifferent, aloof, distant?

Instead of these responses, I can strengthen myself without turning my back on who I am. I become truly stronger when I embrace my sensitivities instead of dismissing them out of shame or fear; when I use challenges to enhance my natural coping mechanisms; when I practice self-care. I can then become a stronger, improved version of myself and re-emerge: still me, but more resilient. Stronger is not being insensitive to pain but able to see through it. I aim for my soft heart to grow stronger. In the meantime, I keep falling, recovering and moving on.

To strengthen myself further, I pay attention to early signs of discomfort, which point out that something bothers me. The earlier I notice, the better. If something feels unsettling, I don't dismiss it. I don't pretend it is not there. Instead, I investigate and release it again and again until it is gone. This leaves me with one trouble less. I also continue widening my perception. The world around me keeps moving at its own pace, but the impact on me is less when I perceive things differently. Having a better grasp of what is going on makes me a more resilient person.

# 14
# Story 14: I Have So Many Problems

A re they even real? I ask myself: "What is my biggest problem right now, this minute, this moment?" More often than not the answer is "none." Yesterday, I had a bothersome tummy ache for a few hours. It was indeed a problem. The evening before, I went to bed thinking I hadn't done as much work as I would have liked. This is not really a problem *unless I make it so*.

Ten years ago, when I took a routine blood test, my serum iron levels appeared to be alarmingly low. I panicked. The doctor was reassuring. He said: "Don't worry so much. We'll deal with it. You must have had this problem for years. You are worried because you've just found out about it. You had this condition yesterday, a month ago and last year, and you weren't concerned. Worrying won't make it go away faster. Come back in a week, and we'll sort it out."

He was right. The problem had been there for a long time. I hadn't been worried because I didn't know. It was *finding out* about it that caused anxiety, not the iron deficiency itself. Discovering it when I did was a blessing because I had the opportunity to fix it. The serum iron deficiency could lead to all sorts of problems, but none of these potential problems was a problem *yet*. They belonged to the future. They did not exist in the present.[11] Taking decisive action instead of worrying prevents problems occurring. To declutter my mind from continuously thinking about problems, I devote time to figuring out practical corrective or preventive actions and practice mind decluttering.

Sometimes my problem is that a loved one has a problem. It is not my problem, but it is equally important to me. If it is a health issue, I do my best to help. Otherwise, I can offer support, practical assistance and advice. I can hold space for them, but I can't solve other people's problems without their contribution. If my help is declined, the only thing I can do is respect that and let that person be while continuing to send them love.

Some problems are choices: hanging out with people that deplete or mistreat me, staying with an abusive partner or putting up with disrespectful behavior. In those cases, I don't have a problem; I am creating one. The solution is entirely up to me. I just have to do myself a favor and get out of the situation.

# 15
# Story 15: I Have No Choice

*I*phigenia at Aulis[12] is an ancient Greek drama written by Euripides in 406 BC. According to the story,
Agamemnon, the king of Mycenae, was the leader of
the Greek coalition during the Trojan War. Before the
war began, the Greek fleet was stranded at the port
of Aulis due to unfavorable weather conditions and
could not set sail to Troy. Agamemnon sought the
counsel of prophet Calchas. He was informed that
the goddess Artemis had sent bad weather because
Agamemnon had offended her. To appease the goddess, the prophet said King Agamemnon should
sacrifice his daughter, Iphigenia. Iphigenia and her
mother begged Agamemnon to spare the girl's life,
but he thought he had no choice. The story ends with
Iphigenia being led (willingly) to her death.

Agamemnon believed he had no choice, and we think the same way when at least one of our options is unbearably harsh. Still, it *is* a choice. Agamemnon could have chosen his daughter over his duty as a leader. Perhaps he would have been dishonored by his allies, but every choice has its consequences. His choice to sacrifice his daughter led to his wife's resentment. Agamemnon survived a ten-year war in Troy, then as soon as he victoriously returned home, his wife had him murdered.

We have a choice even when we think we don't. Taking a specific course of action is a choice. Doing nothing is also a choice. Staying stuck or procrastinating are choices, albeit not very empowered ones. Agamemnon's life could have turned out differently had he made an alternative choice. Maybe he could have found another way to appease Artemis. Maybe not. Perhaps, instead of his wife killing him, he would have been dethroned or disgraced, yet lived to die an old man.

I find owning my choices empowering. Some of them turn out alright and I enjoy the results. Some turn out wrong and I regret them. In either case, it is *I* who has led myself there, so complaining doesn't help. Instead, I can do my best to contain any painful and damaging repercussions. To do that effectively and efficiently, I need to appreciate that these consequences are links in a chain of events that *I* have created or allowed to happen, consciously or unconsciously. When I am struggling to amend my mistakes while at the same time beating myself up, my energy and effort are divided in two. When I accept what is going on, I can focus on corrections more constructively, efficiently and effectively.

Agamemnon had a choice: to be a protective father or a diligent leader. He chose the second. Who can judge him? Our choices are personal because they reflect our priorities at a certain point in life. I usually sacrifice work over family time, but when I am finishing up a project, I may choose to do things the other way round. I can make a different choice every time according to the circumstances and my assessment of the situation.

Choice is arguably our most valuable gift, but we don't always make conscious use of it. We sometimes allow others to decide for us. One of these other decision makers is our subconscious. More often than we think, we allow it to override our free will. The subconscious makes its own choices based on our survival instincts, its imprinted patterns of behavior and its preferences. These are what our subconscious thinks we need, but they may not always be what we want. I often dream of making drastic changes to my life, but I don't materialize them. Whereas my mind knows this is what I want, my subconscious fears change. What if it doesn't work out? What if it backfires? What if I hurt or offend someone? How about waiting for another year? I procrastinate and remain stuck. My subconscious fear of change has chosen for me. In this case, my subconscious works against me. If I want to materialize my conscious choice, I need to discover what is subconsciously holding me back. I can release it if I want and move on.

Sometimes the subconscious knows us better than we think we know ourselves. It works *for* us behind the scenes. Workaholics (including me, on occasion) constantly have pressing work to do. There are always deadlines, clients, meetings and problems to be solved. We keep complaining and we often feel guilty of neglecting friends, family and ourselves. Often, the reason we are so busy all the time is because we either like it—even though we don't admit this even to ourselves—or we are (unknowingly) reluctant to dedicate time to other life roles. The subconscious, knowing our predispositions, keeps finding excuses for us to continue doing what feels most comfortable: working. Acknowledging this, we can either accept that this is who we are and be happy with ourselves or clear the obstacles preventing us from enjoying other aspects of life.

When we are not thriving, it is because we are not choosing to tirelessly work toward this goal. Sticking to it requires effort in overcoming impediments such as debilitating beliefs, damaging habits and disempowering patterns of behavior. It is easier said than done, but it *can* be done.

How?

# PART TWO
## RESTORING

We are born innocent and full of potential. We then learn to be otherwise. What does it take to restore our innocence and regain our power?

Part Two is about rebooting our system and reviewing how we experience life. To do this, we first need to reset our software. We clear old programs imprinted in our subconscious by challenging our self-imposed limitations and letting obsolete, incapacitating beliefs go. We then install a new program. It is not really new; it is the default program we've overwritten with junk along the way. In reclaiming it, we open up to more empowering versions of ourselves and recall our unlimited potential. We then restart our Central Processing Unit: the subconscious. It can now operate differently.

Part Two includes a collection of realizations and practices I use to cut the cords that keep me tied to disempowering nonsense stories. I have learned a lot from my teachers, coaches and mentors around the world. I have combined this knowledge to create an all-encompassing experience. By no means are these practices a panacea. They are examples of how to remove the blinders and allow light through.

# 16

# Perceiving

We keep in contact with the world through our senses, but we can only perceive what we are conditioned (by manufacturing) and trained (by practice) to perceive. The human ear responds to frequencies from 20 Hz to 20,000 Hz.[13] Sound waves are vibrations or patterns of disturbance caused by the movement of energy traveling through a medium. Many more vibrations outside our auditory ability exist, corresponding to frequencies lower or higher than our auditory range, regardless of whether we can hear them. Occasionally, we come across people who can hear a broader range of frequencies due to minuscule differences in the structure of their ears. Others have trained themselves to distinguish subtle differences in sounds missed by most of us, such as the rich vocabulary of birds. Our auditory experience is unique.

The human eye can see a range of wavelengths in the electromagnetic spectrum from about 400 to 700 nanometers.[14] What lies outside this spectrum is invisible to most of us. Visual ability varies greatly among the population, with visual aids such as glasses and contact lenses widely used to adjust and improve eyesight. Some people can see in the dark better than others. The line between what is visible and what is not is somewhat blurred.

Nerve receptors on the skin detect the sensation of making contact with a surface and trigger the sense of touch. The number of receptors and the sensitivity of touch varies from person to person.[15] The sense of touch also depends on how the brain has been trained to interpret the signals received by the receptors.[16] Touch can be refined through practice.[17]

Taste sensitivity depends on the number of flavor receptors in our taste buds and the number of taste buds on the tongue. The amount of flavor receptors varies from person to person,[18] which means our response to what tastes good and what does not, which tastes are strong and which are mild, varies. This explains the reason I love curry while the rest of my family don't.

A smell is experienced when an odorous molecule binds to a receptor within the nasal cavity. It then transmits an electrical signal through the olfactory system to the brain. Millions of olfactory receptor neurons act as sensory signal cells in a human nose. This allows for variances in what we identify as a strong, mild, pleasant or unpleasant odor;[19] thus we have different smell preferences and tolerances. While most people love perfumes, I usually flush them down the drain.

We perceive the world through our hardware and software: how our body is built and what we have programmed or trained it to recognize and react to. Our perception of the world varies and is, in any case, limited. There are too many things going on around us that we don't grasp, can't explain and are not consciously aware of—happenings we can't see, hear, touch, smell or taste that naturally occur and undoubtedly exist. There are places on Earth, Planets in our solar system, and galaxies we have never seen. We don't necessarily dispute their existence: perhaps someone else has seen them or found out about them. There are molecules and atoms, electrons, protons, neutrons, quarks and more vibrating, orbiting and dancing within and around us all the time. They are too small for us to see but they are there. With our restricted abilities of perception, we only perceive part of this Cosmos.

## Taking past experiences for granted

We typically depend on other people's observations and conclusions, from the simplest things to the most complicated ones. I believe the Earth orbits around the Sun and not the other way round, even though I haven't actually *seen* it and my math is not advanced enough to *prove* it. I trust Nicolaus Copernicus[20] and the myriad of physicists and astronomers who advocate their case based on observations, calculations and deductions. Learning from the successes and failures of others has saved humanity a lot of effort, time and resources. It's a shortcut we take all the time.

Even though this is often helpful, there are so many accumulated conclusions in the world that, inevitably, some are junk. Whereas some experiences lead to objective deductions—if I melt ice, I get water—some lead to subjective conclusions: if my partner leaves me, I'll never fall in love again. Such a statement may hold for hundreds or thousands of people, but it is still subjective. It is not *always* so.

Learning from the experience of others what happens if I melt ice is useful. Drawing from the experiences of my broken-hearted teenage friends may not be so. It may spare me sorrow, but it may also prevent me from eventually becoming happy. It can keep me stuck by subconsciously shaping one or more invalid underlying beliefs in my system: that I am unlovable, that I've missed my chance in love, that there is only one perfect fit for each person, that broken hearts don't mend. It is possible that such a belief will affect my mentality, actions and life approach until it is validated. It becomes my reality because I have programmed myself for it.

Associating an occurrence with only one possible outcome is limiting. In science, a successful experiment is typically preceded by many failed ones. If something has failed once, it doesn't mean that it will always fail. There are so many parameters influencing the outcome that slightly changing one may give rise to different results. As dynamic beings living in a constantly shifting Universe where circumstances change every second, what may look like duplication at first glance may turn out differently.

Taking all past experiences for granted is restrictive. Being naive or reckless and ignoring the lessons of the past is dangerous. Balancing experience with possibility is smart. To survive, we need to be cautious. To thrive, we want to seize opportunities. To learn from the past, we look back into the accumulated knowledge of humankind. To find opportunities, we look ahead to the future. We meet in the present.

## Expanding perception

Perception is the process through which we become aware of and interpret external stimuli. It is a neurophysiological process: our ability to see, hear or otherwise become aware of those stimuli through our senses. It is also a conceptual process: how we comprehend and interpret these external stimuli.[21]

We are constantly using an inseparable combination of sensory input and cognitive interpretation: we first *sense* the world, and we then seek to *interpret* that input using our mental and emotional filters—a frame of mind based on concepts. Our filters are what we have trained them to be. They are biased. Sometimes this is good for us. It protects us from a venomous reptile, a busy road, a poisonous gas. The mind recalls that such an experience has previously led to trouble, and it alerts us. Sometimes, though, bias doesn't work in our best interests. We get offended when someone criticizes us, even though ignoring them would be better for us. The mind remembers a past time when we were belittled and how hurtful that was. It gets our defense mechanisms going.

We call others narrow-minded if they don't seem to appreciate a new (or our) way of thinking. Since there are limits to our perception, aren't we all narrow-minded to an extent? To create a tiny fissure in the trained mind's bias we need to recognize that most of our current behavior is based on subjective conclusions and experience.

As much as I would like to consider myself open-minded, I *am* biased. This leaves me with two options: reduce or shift the bias.

To *reduce* my mind's bias, I expand my perception. I embrace there being more to what I can currently perceive. Things are not necessarily this or that way. What I see is just the view from where I stand.

To *shift* the mind's bias, I accept that my imagination often makes things much worse than they really are or will ever be. If half of my problems are created by my mind,[22] it's up to me to change this. I can choose to use my imagination to create positive endings to stories not yet written.

I expand my perception in five ways:

1. By clearing mental space—by letting go

2. By reducing the weight of my beliefs

3. By taking in other peoples' perspectives

4. By exploring my uncensored thoughts and emotions

5. By trying things on, playing them out, giving them a chance

## 1. Clearing mental space—letting go

When the mind is crowded with rigid, pre-existing beliefs, fixations and obsessions, its ability to absorb anything new is significantly reduced. When I try to install new software on my computer when the hard disk is already full, I get a message such as: "Installation not completed. Please free up disk space." If there is to be any chance of something new getting in, I need to make space in my mind by wiping out what has been superseded, what is obsolete, invalid, misleading, outdated and destructive. Once there is space, new entries in the form of concepts, ideas, observations, conclusions, alternatives and possibilities may set in. I clear my memory disk by loosening the ties to the beliefs held in my system.

A loose belief is based on observation: when A happens, B usually follows. A tight belief is based on conviction: every time A happens, B always follows. Convictions are deeply rooted and hard to get rid of; loose beliefs can be pulled out more quickly and easily if I decide to remove those that no longer suit me.

To loosen my beliefs, I question them:

- How have I acquired this belief? When? From whom?

- Is it always so?

- Does it feel right?

- Do I want to keep it?

- Could it be otherwise?

By questioning my belief system, I allow my beliefs to change, and I can let them go.

Putting everyone else first is a thinking pattern I learned from my mother. She never explicitly advised me to think this way, but this is what she did herself. I was taught by example. My mom probably learned it from her own mother, who was observing *her* mother and so forth. As far as I know, I come from a lineage of caring, compassionate women who put everybody else's needs first. The questions are: "Do I agree with this? Do I want to keep this characteristic and pass it on to my daughters, or do I want to drop the relay and choose a different path?"


## 2. Reducing the weight of my beliefs

A heavy belief is one I vow to always hold and comply with; for example, I will never, ever, ever tell a lie. Occasionally, I do lie. I prefer not to, but I sometimes do. I have lied to my children when their pets died, to my teacher when she asked if we liked the lesson, to a colleague about his haircut. Most of these lies I don't regret; I would probably repeat them. A light belief is one I choose to live by, knowing it may not be the only way; for example, I'd rather be truthful. I know I sometimes won't be. I am not obsessed about it.

Heavy beliefs weigh me down. My system becomes bulky, hard, harsh and brittle. It is not friendly to me or anybody else. Making a belief lighter means not sticking to it merely for the sake of it. Every rule has exceptions, and no two situations are identical. Making pompous declarations, such as "I will always speak my mind," may not be a good idea. Sometimes it is better to keep my mouth shut.

To reduce the weight of my beliefs I allow myself to make choices on a case-by-case basis.

## 3. Taking in other people's perspectives

I want to know how other people think. Not to copy them but to see through their eyes. Perhaps they see differently. I respect what seems to be the contrary opinion and accept its potential to be valid. I admit that what I know is a tiny fraction of all that is. I read voraciously. Why not capitalize on other people's findings if they resonate with me? I look for similarities between today's world and ancient civilizations. Early cultures, in their primitive simplicity, were more open-minded than us in some respects. They had fewer years of collective historical bias burdening their minds.

## 4. Exploring my uncensored thoughts and emotions

I rarely get upset anymore, but I used to be a champion at it. To work on this, I find three steps helpful. Step one, I notice it. Step two, I admit it. Step three, instead of avoiding being upset, I look beyond the trigger to find the root cause. This process helps me get to know myself better and deal with what comes up more efficiently and effectively. Being honest with myself is one of the most difficult things I've ever had to do. I was so used to denying my emotions for the sake of how I *wanted* to feel, how I thought I *should* be, how I believed I *ought* to act, that I lost sight of them. They were still there, but I couldn't get in touch with them because I had trained myself to ignore them.

## 5. Trying things on, playing them out and giving them a chance

This approach has helped me find what I wholeheartedly enjoy and what I don't. Unless I give something a shot, how will I know whether I like it or not? How will I ever find out whether I would have been good at it?

Perception is a muscle. We can train it in the same way we exercise the body. This requires noticing and challenging how we respond to external stimuli. By persistently stretching perception, we can comprehend and experience what untrained people can't, just as Olympic athletes can use their bodies in ways not everyone can.

---

## EXPERIMENT 1: OBSERVING

For a week, practice observing rather than assuming. Drop the drama and see what is happening. Instead of jumping to conclusions, getting worked up or taking sides, allow yourself to be a witness. Being an observer of events, occurrences and behaviors (including our own) feels better than judging. It is also informative. Perhaps what was frustrating becomes interesting; anger is replaced by curiosity and compassion; victimization gives way to appreciation of how things are, how life can be and how we are all shaped and conditioned. Everything looks clearer from the observer's point of view.

Every time you catch yourself thinking or behaving in a way that is based on assumptions or arbitrary deductions, pause, and ask yourself: "Am I being tortured by unjustified fears because I can't see things, people and situations as they are—available, harmless and malleable? Am I missing opportunities because I am ruling out possibilities?" Giving up assumptions helps us gain awareness.

During my week of not assuming, I happened to be waiting at a long airport queue. I had been there for almost an hour when a man skipped the line and went straight to the front. Assuming he wanted to circumvent the rest of us, my impulse was to grab him by the lapel and bring him back in line. Instead, I made eye contact with him and waved a question mark. He politely gestured for my patience. A couple of minutes later, he walked up to me to apologize. He said he just wanted to make sure he was waiting at the right counter. Talking to him I realized that *I* had been queuing at the wrong place all along and I immediately sought the right desk. I barely caught my flight.

Less is more. Less assuming reduces mistakes and heightens perception, awareness and efficiency.

---

# Summary

- How we interpret the world and make sense of it depends on our conditioning and past experience. By fine-tuning our senses and detaching from convictions, we can perceive the world in a different way.

- Learning from the experience of others can be beneficial, but let's not allow this to limit us.

- We can expand our perception by:

  - Reducing the rigidness of our beliefs.

  - Appreciating other people's perspectives.

  - Paying attention to our thoughts and emotions.

  - Trying things on.

- In Experiment 1 we discover the benefits of observing rather than assuming.

# 17
# Intuiting

If we believe we only have access to what we can see, hear, taste, smell and touch, we are greatly underestimating ourselves. We receive information through every cell of our physical body and our energy space, our personal Flight Information Region (FIR). In aviation, airspace is divided into FIRs, where flight information and alerting services are available.[23] Through these services, aircraft receive information on the traffic and weather in their vicinity. Similarly, the space around me contains an abundance of data. It is up to me to tap into it and receive the available information, stimuli and alerts. A broadened perception works like an X-ray device. It enables us to see *into* situations and recognize what is not evident at first glance. We can then read between the lines and see behind the images. We can penetrate through words, lies and excuses. We can perceive past pretexts and pretenses.

We can further broaden perception by training one more sense: intuition, the so-called sixth sense. There is nothing new, weird or supernatural about this. Individuals throughout human history and across cultures have been training and refining their senses, achieving extraordinary results. We all have intuition, but sometimes, when it warns us about something, we choose to ignore it. We convince ourselves that it is nonsense. We deny its existence. As a result, it gradually weakens and eventually stops contributing to our lives.

## The clairs

What some people call the "clairs" are our six senses sharpened and cleared of distortion or interference that gets in the way of sensing.[24] Originating from the word "clarity," a clair allows a clearer intake of sensory stimuli:

- **Clairvoyance** stands for clear vision: images flash through our mind's eye, our third eye, concerning the past, present or future.

- **Clairaudience** is for clear hearing: we hear words, sounds or music within our own mind.

- **Clairtangency** translates as clear touch: by touching a person, a plant, an animal or an object, important information is conveyed about their history or emotional state.

- **Clairalience** or **clairscentence** means clear smelling: the ability to smell odors that don't seem to have a physical source.

- **Clairgustance** is clear tasting: being able to taste something that has not come into physical contact with our tongue or mouth.

- **Clairsentience** corresponds to a clear feeling of another person's emotions. **Claircognizance** means clear knowing: having nonlocal knowledge about people or events. This means possessing information we couldn't possibly know. **Clairempathy** is sensing another person's physical pain or discomfort.

To enjoy a clearer intake of sensory stimuli, we need to train our sensory equipment. We can train one, several or all senses to a higher clarity. Once initiated, these sensitivities grow not by learning new skills, but by *unlearning* stereotypes, dogmas and patterns of interpretation that may be standing in the way of receiving pure, uncensored external data precisely as it is. We allow ourselves to sense more deeply without letting the mind interfere.

An example of this in its simplest form would be my mind telling me there will be no vacant parking space at the mall on a Saturday morning, and my intuition informing me that on Level 2 of the multistory car park there are a couple of spots left. Occasionally, my clairvoyance shows me where the vacant spot is— next to a red van or between two black SUVs on the north side, in Section B. If I trust it and go directly there, I find the available spot. If I ignore it or linger looking elsewhere (which means that I doubt it), I have a harder time finding a parking place.

## A higher awareness

I am walking down the street distracted, thinking of nothing in particular. My mind is taking a break. Suddenly, a thought strikes me, and I know beyond doubt that *this* is the answer to a problem that has been bothering me for days. How do I know? I just do. The pieces of the puzzle finally fit together. It feels like the answer has been there all along, but it has only just dawned on me. I think: "AHA! I got ya!"

Sound familiar?

These AHAs! are moments of experiencing **A Higher Awareness**. We all get them, but we don't recognize them, either because we are not paying attention or because we are used to having them. My AHA!s are among my most important assets. They pop up when least expected, offer solutions and contribute to my wellbeing. Historical AHA!s make some of the world's most inspiring stories.

## Eureka!

While taking his bath at a public spa, ancient physicist Archimedes (287–212 BC), realized that when an object is immersed in water (or any fluid) it is buoyed up by a force equal to the weight of the water displaced by the object.[25] Archimedes was so excited about his discovery that he got out of the bathtub and ran naked out of the spa, screaming "Eureka: I found it!" That particular incident of higher awareness was a crucial milestone for science.

## Ouch!

Isaac Newton (1642–1726 AD) put together the theory of gravity when allegedly an apple fell on his head.[26] He had an AHA! just like Chicken Little, in Story 1. Newton's quest started by wondering what made the apple fall straight down, rather than sideways or even upward. He was later able to show that the force that makes the apple fall and holds us on the ground is the same force that keeps the Moon and Planets in orbit.

Prominent physicists, scientists, philosophers and inventors had similar AHA!s when they arrived at their most profound breakthroughs. What their stories have in common is that *first* the revelation came to them, *then* they articulated their theory and *lastly* they proved it, rather than the other way round.[27] They had A Higher Awareness. They saw a hidden truth. They drilled deeper into their perception. These people were not only intelligent but also curious. They challenged what was, until then, widely accepted. They had vivid imaginations. They believed in the magic of the Universe. They embraced what seemed irrational. They trusted in possibility. They allowed awareness to flow through. They realized that "maybe" meant "it *may*—actually—*be*."

In the Middle Ages, physical phenomena, such as magnetism, and inventions, such as electricity, were considered black magic. The majority of people were not ready to engage with something that had existed in nature for billions of years but didn't make sense to them and their limited perception. However, it made perfect sense to a handful of pioneers. We now know better, but how would we have reacted back then? How many current ideas, experiences or AHA!s do we dismiss, frown upon or laugh at?

My AHA!s confirm to me that my perception is indeed expanding. When they occur, it feels like I am unlocking a door, stepping into a vast empty space. As they begin to sink in, I become less attached to presumptions, convictions and opinions. I can tolerate and even be amused with conversations, thoughts and ideas that would normally drive me up the wall. This makes life easier for me and those around me.

To allow the influx of awareness and to increase my AHA!s, I establish quietness. There is usually too much noise and fog in our minds and hearts, arising from anger, rejection, constraints, restraints, comparisons, should be's, would be's, could be's. Such concerns often create so much interference and distraction that useful signals can't get through. The answer is in front of us, but we can neither see nor hear it.

# Summary

- Intuition, our sixth sense, is usually underused and dormant. We can train it to provide us with insights and valuable information related to our lives.

- The "clairs" are our six senses sharpened so that we can perceive the world more deeply and meaningfully.

- An AHA! is more than a random thought that shows up. It is **A Higher Awareness**: our ability to reach deeper levels of perception for a moment.

# 18
# Aligning Life With The Laws Of Nature

Many of us believe that nature has its rules and we make our own. A broadened perception allows for a different perspective. Whether we like it or not, no matter how many rules and regulations we establish, we are an inseparable part of the Cosmos. If we analyze our individual, unique behavior and how our reality unfolds, we arrive at the same principles that apply to nature, the world around us and the Universe as a coherent system. We realize we are *part* of nature. Our emotional and behavioral patterns mimic physical phenomena and follow the same fundamental natural laws. From a cell, the tiniest form of life, to our colossal Universe itself, everything is born, lives and dies.

So how does this apply to our lives?

# Learning from the Universe

To compensate for our limited perception, we invest in science to comprehend what is happening around us. Science explains the physical phenomena we have managed to decode, the physics we know; but there is much more to physics than that—there is everything we haven't yet figured out. What if we could use the knowledge we have acquired about the world around us to make sense of what is going on inside us, how our own lives play out and how to improve them? We can learn about ourselves from the fundamentals of the Universe.

## Randomness

Most mathematicians, statisticians, physicists, scientists, engineers and researchers agree that nothing in our Universe is random.[28] What *seems* random is, in fact, a pattern we haven't worked out yet. This assures me that there is a purpose to everything, including me and my life. It also motivates me to pay attention to what is happening to me and around me. If nothing is random and there is a reason for everything, then whatever I am experiencing now is the effect of something that has already happened. It has a cause.

## Time

The sequential nature of cause and effect makes time possible.[29] *First* I cut my finger, *then* it bleeds. It can't be the other way round. Decisions and actions lead to results, and this sequence creates my experience of time. It also provides a practical framework within which I can trace occurrences back to their root causes and make effective changes.

## Energy and matter

For a long time, we thought matter and energy were two different concepts. Then Albert Einstein and his relativity theory turned the world upside down.[30] We *are* energy. This is not religion or philosophy. It's physics. It is also a life-changing revelation. If I perceive myself as a big chunk of stagnant material—a body— it is hard for me to overcome obstacles, make fast changes and recuperate from hardship and illness. If I recognize that I am a vibrating energetic being, a cluster of tirelessly oscillating particles, everything becomes easier. I can facilitate and expedite change, personal growth and healing.

## Entropy

As our Universe keeps expanding, the energy within it is neither created nor lost. It is transformed from one type of energy to another, while the total energy in the Universe remains constant. This is the principle of conservation of energy, the first law of thermodynamics, and it also holds for information.[31] Concentrated or dispersed, all the information we need is somewhere out there, but as the Universe expands and information is scattered into a larger volume of three-dimensional space (or area of a possibly two-dimensional Universe), it becomes harder for us to access. Information isn't lost, but entropy—the degree of disorder—is increasing.[32] This means less information is available in each cubic meter of space (or square meter in the Universe).

Many years ago, on a rainy afternoon, I was leisurely sipping coffee, keeping an eye on a group of six-year-olds playing board games on my living room floor. When the rain stopped, they stormed outside. I abandoned my coffee and ran around the garden, ensuring they were safe. As the space available to the kids grew, they found more things to do and more places to be. The level of disorder rose, and I lost my peace of mind. This is how entropy increases and energy and information are scattered in our expanding Universe. Hence the reason life is becoming more complicated even though science and technology are advancing. Quietness, wisdom and balance are increasingly hard to find.

## Energy packs

We used to think of the physical world as a continuum: a progression of sequential elements that vary imperceptibly. Then quantum physicists told us we may have been wrong. Radiation is quantized: it comes in discrete batches of energy, or energy packs.[33] Just as a seemingly continuous ray of light is in fact made up of sequential energy packs, I can envision my life as a sequence of discrete stories instead of a single life story. These unique, dependent or independent, sequential stories make up my exclusive storyline. Living through distinct stories reminds me that my life story is neither rigid nor predetermined. This offers me the opportunity to:

- Choose the stories I want to experience over those I'd rather avoid

- Rewrite stories that have a poor track record and change their plots, chapters, characters and endings to make them happier

- Reduce the impact of painful past stories on my present and future

- Write new stories for myself and for the generations to come

- Live parallel stories and make the most of my time

When I perceive life in the form of discrete stories, I can leave a story behind, skip one altogether and select a new one while creating my own narrative. I can de-compose old stories and re-story them differently, using—as much as possible—the fundamental laws of physics.

## Cause and effect

It is often said there is no smoke without fire, and the following account of a personal incident illustrates this.

In 1997 I was living in an eight-apartment building. My roommates had gone home for the summer and I was the only one in the apartment. Many people were away for the holidays and the place was quiet. I was usually careful to shut the building's front entrance behind me when going out. That day, I didn't hear the familiar *click*, but I didn't go back to check. I could already see my bus arriving at the bus stop and I didn't want to be late for work. I anxiously ran across the street and barely caught the bus. I put my hand in my pocket, searching for a ticket, only to realize I had left the stack of bus tickets on the kitchen counter. I cowered in a corner, hoping it was too early in the morning for an inspector to show up. It wasn't. A couple of stops later, an inspector boarded the bus and fined me. "Well deserved," I thought to myself.

On the way home that evening, I caught sight of a sock on the pavement outside my building. That sock was unmistakably mine. Something was wrong. I ran up the stairs, my heart racing. The door to my apartment was missing. Someone had broken in and the apartment was a mess. I looked for my laptop. It was gone. Thankfully, my roommates had locked their rooms before leaving and the intruder hadn't broken into their bedrooms. Apart from my computer, there didn't seem to be a substantial loss of valuables.

All my clothes had been thrown on the floor. No wonder my socks were all over the neighborhood. My personal space—my sanctuary—had been violated. The police came and took fingerprints. I spent the night on the couch, staring at the gap where the apartment door had been. Over the next couple of days, I had the door fixed, cleaned the apartment and did laundry. I was shaken but—at the same time— relieved that nobody else in the building had incurred any damages due to my stupidity. I had made a mistake. I hadn't securely closed the front door that morning and there were repercussions. There was cause and effect.

I was partly responsible for what happened that day. Action—and nonaction—bears consequences. The reason I can't always see this is my limited perception. From where I stand, I cannot easily connect the dots and make out the patterns. Appreciating the validity of the principle of cause and effect helps me accept downfalls, even though I don't like them, and I can make sense of what happens. I could have blamed the bus inspector for fining me, but *I* was the one who had forgotten my ticket. She was doing her job. I was also responsible for securely closing the building's entrance behind me. I hadn't. My carelessness doesn't justify the burglar, but it made the burglary easier. I had played my part.

## Assuming responsibility

Acknowledging the principle of cause and effect helps me assume responsibility for myself. Responsibility starts with adulthood. No child can be held accountable for how their parents treat them. When we are young, dependent individuals, it is difficult to distinguish our emotions from those of our caregivers. Becoming an adult means gaining control and finding ways to overcome whatever happened to us as children. Living responsibly means no matter what happened yesterday and for whatever reason, today I have a choice to start getting over it. Horrible things may have taken place, but it is my responsibility toward myself to seek help, find ways to heal and leave them behind. This is not always easy to do but no one else will or can do it for me.

Assuming responsibility means:

- Knowing where I stand. I no longer need to make Mommy or Daddy accountable for inherited health problems and acquired disempowering thinking patterns. I recognize I haven't inherited defects but rather a belief system from my family. It is my job to change it if I want to.

- Not blaming others. I don't need to blame the economy for my investments going down, my partner if I feel neglected, my children when I am exhausted or my boss when I am having a hard time at work. I can stop being passive and I can take action. I can decide that from now on my choices are my responsibility. Even when I give everything up for someone else's sake, this is still *my* choice.

- Refusing to make excuses. There is a big difference between a cause and an excuse. When I make excuses, I am trying to absolve responsibility for my actions because I feel insecure about myself, guilty for my choices or fearful of being judged. Refusing to work through a painful or traumatic experience is an excuse that I make to postpone taking control and ownership of my life.

- Admitting my mistakes, yet forgiving myself. Acknowledging that I did something wrong is an internal process. Regardless of whether I admit it out loud, the least I can do is admit it to myself. I can then work on releasing guilt and self-blame. There is a thin line between recognizing my mistake yet forgiving myself and making up a pile of excuses trying to convince myself that it wasn't my fault.

- Appreciating that I am the creator of my emotions and the person solely responsible for them. When I get offended, I ask myself: "Has this person stirred an insecurity in me?" When envious, I question: "Am I comparing myself to someone?" When irritated, I ask: "Are my buttons being pushed?" When defensive, I wonder: "Do I feel threatened?" These are *my* emotions, and I am the only one qualified to dissolve them.

Assuming responsibility is liberating. I am replacing victim with victor. Even when I don't know who I am, I know who I am not. I am not a victim of circumstance, a prey or a casualty. I can't control everything that happens, but I *can* control my choices. Pretty or ugly, they are mine.

Accepting ownership and self-responsibility is a lonely game, but it's the price to pay for being in power. To accomplish it, I need to be aware of what is going on with me. I do this by asking questions.

## Summary

- Life mimics nature and the laws of physics apply to our emotional world and our everyday reality.

- We can use fundamental principles of physics to make sense of our life.

- In nature, occurrences are the effects of causes. Similarly, in life, whatever happens is a result of something that preceded it.

- Understanding the principle of cause and effect helps us assume responsibility for ourselves.

# 19

# Investigating Through Personal Q&A Sessions

Nasreddin Hodja was a Sufi philosopher known for his amusing didactic stories. The following story is attributed to him.

In the middle of the night, a man is looking for something on the ground. A patrolling policeman stops. "Do you need any help?" he asks.

"Yes, my friend. I am looking for my keys. Can you please help me find them?"

Both men search for the keys for a while. The policeman then asks the man: "Do you remember roughly where you dropped them?"

"Yes! Sure! You see those trees over there?" the man replies, pointing to the nearby park. The policeman looks at him, puzzled.

"If you have lost them over there, why are you looking for them here?"

"Because the streetlamp shines much better here."[34]

This is the streetlight effect. Like the man in the story, I am often looking for answers in the wrong place. No wonder I don't find them. I also sometimes experience intense emotions under seemingly irrelevant circumstances. When this happens, it is not the current situation I need to address but what this situation is triggering. Unaddressed emotions, like unfinished business and old debts, may hibernate for a long time, but they don't go away. Instead, they are stirred by relevant or irrelevant occurrences; they repeat as patterns, or they show up uninvited when least expected. To find out the root causes of my beliefs, emotions and behavior, I need to pose the right questions.

## The art of asking questions

We ask questions to get answers. The smarter the question, the more meaningful the answer. Asking "why" is tricky, because it leads me to vague, impractical and misleading answers:

- Why can't I figure out how to calculate my taxes? Because I'm stupid. Because it's complicated. Because the idiot who wrote these instructions was clueless.

- Why am I stuck in life? Because I'm a loser. Because life is unfair. Because we all screw up in this family.

I expect answers, but I end up with excuses. There is at least one reason, or cause, for an effect I am experiencing. Unfortunately, there are also hundreds of excuses. Unless I use "why" carefully, it misleads me because it directs me to the excuses instead of the cause. Excuses can't help me find a solution because they are not the real reason for what is happening. I'm wasting my time when I try to solve a problem by addressing the apparent excuses. It disorients me and I stray from the real root cause. It depletes my energy, as I enter a loop of complaining, shaming, blaming and feeling victimized, helpless and hopeless.

"Why" questions are confusing when I use them to obtain information about other people's behavior. For example: "Why is he such a jackass?" "Why is she doing this to me?" I can come up with hundreds of answers. Only a few of them will help me comprehend another person's conduct.

The quality of my questions determines the accuracy and practicality of the answers. Fact-seeking, emotion-free questions (even when investigating my emotions) usually work better.

It was Monday morning, November 1994. I knocked on the door of one of my university lecturers. I had spent the entire weekend unsuccessfully trying to complete my assignment. It was time to ask for help. The professor was available to first-year students every Monday morning, so there I was outside his office for the first time. We exchanged greetings and I got straight to the point.

"Prof, I can't figure out how to solve this problem. I've spent hours on it, but I just don't know why—"

"I am not interested in your problems, young lady," he interrupted me impatiently. I was taken aback.

"I thought you didn't mind helping us with the coursework." I knew that many students had been seeking his help.

"This is true. I am at your disposal. However, I have a rule. I don't offer solutions to students. My lectures end in the lecture theater. In my office, I am open to discussion. If you have a sensible suggestion, we can talk about it."

I explained how I had approached the problem. He asked me one question. As I was working out the answer, I realized what I had been doing wrong. AHA! The answer had been right there in front of me all along. All I had to do was ask myself the right question.

From Confucius and Socrates to Leonardo da Vinci, Mark Twain and Albert Einstein, deep thinkers had something in common. They were curious and asked lots of questions.[35] They were not interested in other people's business but in how the world is and how it functions. Scientists, philosophers, inventors and innovators consider, discuss, test, validate or invalidate ideas:

- Where does this lead?

- What happens when these two elements interact?

- How can I make this work?

When I want to solve a problem or find an answer, I take time to brainstorm. I pose questions. I avoid asking why. Instead, I work with the rest of the question words:

- When did this belief first show up? In 2005/on my first day at school.

- Who was I with? Mom/Dad/my first-grade teacher/by myself.

- Where was I? At home/at school/camping.

- What was I doing? Trying to help/my homework/hanging out with my friends.

- What happened? I overheard them say I'm a loser.

- How did it make me feel? Belittled/ashamed/rejected/unloved/lonely.

- Which other occasions evoke(d) a similar emotion? When the teacher scolded me for getting the answers wrong/when my boss reprimands me/when my mate accuses me of being useless.

I allow questions to follow one another. I don't rule out "silly" questions. I follow my instinct. I am curious to see where all this leads, and what it reveals: The root cause of me believing I'm a loser, feeling and behaving like one in almost everything I do is that an important person rejected me many years ago and I bought into it. This belief was rooted in my mind and has been affecting my life ever since.

Any time is a good time to ask questions. When a troublesome emotion or a limiting belief comes up in the middle of a busy day, I make a note to check on it later. I don't postpone it indefinitely. It only takes a few minutes, so I don't use lack of time as an excuse to procrastinate. If I need to schedule meeting time with myself, I do. When calmer and less emotional, I manage to ask more meaningful questions to which I get better answers. However imperfectly I start, asking one question leads to another and I eventually find what I am looking for.

Dedicating time to ask questions, seek answers and clear emotional junk, heaviness and turmoil before it piles up is as essential as taking a daily shower. The point is to keep both my physique and my psyche clean.

---

## EXPERIMENT 2: ASKING QUESTIONS

Dedicate a week to mindfully posing targeted questions and exploring different questioning techniques. Question how you feel or how others behave. What could be the underlying motive? Refrain from asking why and work with the rest of the question words. Once the week is over, you will know which questions work best for you.

With practice, conversing with ourselves efficiently soon becomes a habit. The mind is trained to generate smart and practical questions.

---

## Downloading the answer

Consider this anecdote:

> On a deserted island, a shipwrecked man desperately prays to God.
>
> "Please save me! I believe in you!"
>
> Soon after, a small boat sails by, heading for the mainland. Its crew spot the man on the island and invite him on board.
>
> "From the bottom of my heart I thank you, but there is no need. God will save me."
>
> The boat departs and the man resumes his prayers. A few days later, a seaplane lands close to the island. The pilot offers the man a ride. The man declines.
>
> "Thank you, sir, but I am fine. God will save me. I trust in him."
>
> The seaplane takes off and the man goes back to praying. A week later, a helicopter lands on the beach. A rescue team tries to persuade the exhausted, famished man to board. Once more, he refuses. He has faith. *God* will save him. Shortly after, the man dies. When finally in heaven, he asks God for a private hearing.
>
> "My God, I trusted you and you gave up on me. I prayed to you and you turned your back on me. Why didn't you save me?"
>
> God looks surprised.
>
> "I sent you a sailing boat, a seaplane and a helicopter and every time you declined. What else could I do?"[36]

Asking a good question is half the job. The rest is knowing how to receive the answer recognizing it for what it is. After posing a question, I *allow* answers to come through. No thinking is permitted. I don't try to figure out the answer. If I set my reasoning or guessing mechanisms going, I err. Since the mind is biased by the stories it has been fed, I turn to the clarity of my senses. To prevent my mind from jumping to conclusions, I focus on the present.

Often a picture pops into my head. It may be a person, a place or an experience. At other times a word is written in front of my eyes. It can be a voice of judgment or warning—a parent's, a teacher's, a lover's or a person's I hold accountable for my misery—or the sound of a storm or a siren signifying a shocking or traumatic event. The answer may come as mouth dryness, a sour or bitter flavor, the taste of blood or sand. More rarely, it is an odor: the smell of sweat, fire or gas. It could be the recollection of a sense of touch, a squeeze around the neck, a blade cutting through the heart. It can be the sensation of suffocating, heart racing, head buzzing.

Downloading an answer is simpler than it sounds. It requires trusting the senses and silencing the mind. When doing math, I rely on my mind. When asking personal questions, I have confidence in my senses. They are more accurate in describing how something *is*, whereas the mind tends to think of how it *should be*. Intuition is so gentle and subtle that, as available as it is, it is easy to stray from. My logic, the thinking and assuming part of my brain, can override my intuition and blur it.

Sensory input information is much less censored than my learned thinking patterns. Turning to sensing instead of thinking, I can identify the vibration underlying an experience and determine its quality. Is it loving and nurturing, or fearful and depleting? Senses can more easily connect to the energy that makes up our material world. Energy travels fast. The faster the answer shows up, the more accurate it is. As soon as I pause, I inevitably start thinking and answers become biased. When seeking answers intuitively, the two-second rule applies: unless I get an answer within a couple of seconds, it may not be valid. If the answer is not coming through right away, I let it rest instead of pushing for it. It is possible that the answer will come later in the day, in unexpected forms. A person I meet may tip me off. I may be reading a book or an article and get an AHA! While listening to the radio or watching a movie, what I had been looking for suddenly dawns on me.

A few years ago, I was in a dilemma about whether to attend a workshop in California or one in London. They both looked interesting and promising. On the last day of registrations, I was driving my kids to school, still undecided. I was queuing at the traffic lights when I glanced at the car in front of me. Its number plates read LAX—the abbreviation for Los Angeles International Airport. I went home and registered for the workshop in California. I am grateful that I followed my intuition. On that day and the days that followed, I had many cues confirming my decision.

We often receive these clues. We just don't pay attention. Cues and signs are not generic omens: a black cat, a broken mirror or a crow. Those are superstitions. Meaningful signs include observations and occurrences that are relevant to a decision and either reinforce or contradict it. When I am considering doing something but everything that happens seems to be opposing it, I need to pose a question: "Is this a cue for me to be careful instead of rushing into something?" Or "Are my insecurities rising, preventing me from taking action?" I act according to the answer.

When an answer insists on not showing up, this is also in my best interest. If an answer is not available to me, it doesn't necessarily mean I am doing something wrong. It is possible I am not ready to handle the situation yet. I know this because I occasionally have an intense awareness and struggle to make peace with the information I receive. We all have different levels of understanding at different points in time because we can only perceive what we can deal with. Some things are not easy to conceive and are hard to digest, so it may be better we don't have access to everything at once, as this would be overwhelming. When I have a profound AHA! it seems so clear and obvious that for a moment I wonder how I hadn't realized it before. Then I think of myself a few years or months back, and understand I couldn't have handled it. A self-protection mechanism is in place, preventing my system from overload and burnout.

## Peter versus Peter

Expanding my perception helps me realize how little I know and makes space for what I don't yet comprehend. I know there are things I can't grasp right now. My knowledge is limited, so I keep studying to learn more. When it comes to my intuition, however, the only way to make it work is to unconditionally trust it. Trusting in my intuition is a prerequisite to getting accurate feedback. When my intuition leads me to an answer, this may not be the full answer, but it is part of it and therefore useful. It is perhaps as much as I can handle at the moment. It's a start. It is what I need. Second-guessing myself leads to mistakes. When I lack confidence or I distrust myself, judgments, doubts, insecurities, fears, preferences and biases blur or distort the answer. My intuition weakens.

According to the Bible, when St. Peter saw Jesus walking on the surface of a lake, he became excited and spontaneously rushed to join him. For a moment, he forgot he was a humble fisherman. He achieved a miracle: he was walking on water.[37] He then paused for a split second to consider what he was doing. The tiniest of doubts momentarily crossed his mind, and he sank. This mental process also happens to me. I am a visual person and I often see the answers to my questions forming before me as letters or words. If I judge these images or second-guess their validity, I am misguided. I then realize my mistake and I remember St. Peter. Once more, I have sunk into my own ocean of doubts.

111

The energy I *receive* as a download (the answer) has the same frequency as the *request* I put out in the Universe. If my request is genuine, targeted and confident, so is the answer. If it is forced, stressed and doubtful, the response is of equally poor quality. When I doubt or test myself, I get ambiguous answers.

I *do* make mistakes in my internal Q&As, but it is rarely the disclosure that is wrong. It is mainly an erroneous interpretation on my behalf, because I am either inexperienced or too involved to maintain distance, neutrality and clarity. It can also be because I am holding a piece of the puzzle, but I can't yet figure out where it fits.

While I avoid second-guessing my intuition, I don't want to be stubborn and rigid in my beliefs. Beliefs are fed to the mind from the outside in. They are malleable, interchangeable and biased. It is not unusual to get them mixed up. Intuition works differently. It comes from the inside out. It emerges from a place of purity and neutrality. When I am intuitively seeking an answer, the more neutral I am, the more accurate the answer is. If I pose a question regarding a stranger, I am usually emotionally unattached and I effortlessly receive a clear answer. When intuitively investigating a loved one's concern or one of my own problems, the probability of getting it right decreases. Sometimes my wishful thinking kicks in, sugarcoats the pill and prevents me from seeing what is right in front of me; or my worst fears are stirred up and I falsely pick up the scenario I most dread. This partly explains the reason many energy healers have no trouble healing others but find it difficult to cure themselves. Our objectivity and clarity are impaired.

# Dreaming

Dreams are essential and for good reason. They are stories told by the subconscious, often revealing a concern, a worry, a fear. When I am asleep, my conscious mind is at rest and the subconscious takes over. The stories that unfold relate less to what I *actively* think and more to my deeply imprinted beliefs and anxieties. Acknowledging the emotion *behind* the story in the dream provides me with important information about what is holding me back and what scares me. Addressing these emotions is vital to my wellbeing. When I wake up with a headache, it is often the result of a dream I had during the night. The plot of the dream is not significant; its value is in the emotional state it reveals. My most frequent unpleasant dream is cleaning dirty public toilets. It took me a while to recognize that this was a revelation of my subconsciously held belief that I am responsible for clearing other people's mess and making things right for them.

Instead of relying on generic guidance to explain my dreams and what they may represent, I apply the Q&A process to them. I don't struggle to remember dreams. If I wake up during the night in the middle of an intense dream or if I can remember a dream in the morning, I jot it down in the notepad I keep next to my bed. This way, I can devote time to processing it when I am in the mood. If I can't remember a dream, I don't worry. It will come back if it must.

# Daydreaming

Daydreams reveal what I most desire. When I was little, I used to daydream a lot. I was constantly absent-minded. My body was in one place while my mind was elsewhere. I had imaginary friends, I traveled and lived many different lives, which were more interesting than my real life. However, while daydreaming, I was unknowingly splitting my energy into two: part of it sustained what I was doing and part what I was thinking. It was no surprise I was so inefficient. Daydreaming was stopping me from living in the moment. As the subject of the daydream was usually something I didn't have, daydreaming was also shifting my focus to what I lacked and wholeheartedly wanted.

When I think I don't know what I want, daydreams show me. They are scenes from a movie revealing what I am secretly longing for and how I would like my life to be. Dismissing the daydream, I am probably turning my back on something that could have made me happy. It is a great opportunity lost, especially if I am not satisfied with my current lifestyle. Knowing what I want is a matter of assessing what I can afford financially and logistically. Any step I take, no matter how small, brings me a step closer to achieving those goals.

On the other hand, if I indulge in a daydream without taking conscious action, I am gradually creating a monster, a chimera: a deep illusory desire impossible to achieve. In Greek mythology, Chimera was a hideous creature.[38] She partnered with another beast,

114

Orthrus, and as a result of their genetic combination, their offspring were monstrous and powerful. If I don't actively pursue my (day)dreams, I am feeding the chimera, making it stronger and more aggressive. She and her children—the needs or regrets born inside me—hunt me down and I have a hard time escaping them. "Chasing chimeras" means going after the untouchable: that which cannot be achieved. While daydreaming doesn't necessarily involve something extreme, the subject matter may take on enormous proportions if left unaddressed. Desire magnifies it and it can become an obsession.

Being nostalgic about the past is another kind of daydreaming. Having pleasant memories means I have made some good choices in my life, but if I spend too long reliving them, I get stuck with them. I am missing the present moment and the opportunity to generate more happy memories.

## Summary

- When we are looking in the wrong place, the chances of finding meaningful and helpful answers are low.

- Obtaining useful and practical answers requires smart and effective questioning.

- In Experiment 2, we practice asking meaningful questions about our behavior and the behavior of others, until it becomes a habit.

- Receiving answers intuitively requires us to silence the mind and trust our senses.

- Self-doubt compromises our intuition and makes it difficult to receive accurate answers.

- As dreams tend to reveal our deepest subconscious fears, we can use them to identify and heal these.

- Daydreaming may seem fun, but it is distracting us from living in the present moment. It is useful in that it may reveal deep desires.

# 20

# Paying Attention
# To The Body

When the body speaks, who listens? Body language is a science in itself, and paying attention
to the body is fascinating. There are reasons my body
reacts the way it does to internal and external stimuli.
My body is my compass and I notice the patterns in
its reactions to gain insights into my emotional states.
The two are closely linked, but we haven't learned to
correlate them.

The easiest way to observe my body's behavior is
to notice the contrast between contraction and expansion. My body wants to stretch and expand when I
operate in the emotions of happiness, joy, peace and
love, which carry high vibrations. It feels safe and confident to occupy more space and I feel like shouting
"Yeah, babe!" It is as though I want to make my presence known to the world and claim my ground. I feel

generous and large. Athletes instinctively jump into the air after winning a competition. Runners throw their hands up at the end of a successful race. When basketball players score, they give high fives. Their bodies are saying: "I like this; I'm proud of myself; I am on top of my game." When I feel healthy, content and strong, I want to travel and discover places. This is another form of me stretching. My happy self is expansive. She wants to be on the move.

Sitting on a friend's porch, I watched Simone, the cat, playfully cornering a mouse. Simone had just been fed and was full. She didn't harm the mouse; she just sat there observing it for some time. The mouse froze and shrank into the corner in an effort to pass unnoticed. Simone watched closely. As soon as we distracted her, the mouse disappeared into the bushes. My body also contracts when I operate in the states of anger, fear and remorse, which carry low vibrations. Like a mouse, I cower in the corner, in survival mode, hiding until the danger passes. Without realizing it, I clench my fists and grind my teeth. I cross my arms and legs and instinctively draw them closer to my torso. My breath turns shallow. I am minimizing my spatial exposure. I become smaller and compressed. My body is saying: "I don't like this at all. I don't feel safe. I am exposed." When I am sick, tired or weak, I don't feel like stepping out of my front door. I withdraw into my house and curl up on the couch. My unhappy self is contracting. She wants to isolate herself.

Physical changes in my body give me clues about my psyche. When this happens, I pause and ask questions to find and release the root cause of this emotional reaction. Paying attention to my body's natural response to people and circumstances, I observe that it instinctively contracts in the presence of certain people. For one reason or another it doesn't feel safe. I may not be consciously aware that a specific person sucks my energy or that I shrink in their presence, but my body's unmistakable impulse to defend herself gives me information that my brain is oblivious to. There are other individuals in whose company my body feels like stretching and expanding. I feel safe, comfortable and confident enough to show up as I am. When I force myself to hang out with a person, I can trick my mind, but not my body. If my posture becomes defensive, I know there is no genuine comfort in that encounter, no matter how hard I try. While I can co-exist with this person, they are not my cup of tea.

When my body speaks to me, I want to do myself a favor and listen. I may not always be able to interpret the cues, but I am learning.

---

### EXPERIMENT 3: AT MY BEST AND AT MY WORST

"Mirror, mirror on the wall, what do I look like at my best and my worst?"

Check yourself in the mirror while you are feeling at your best. Re-experience and magnify happy emotions. Re-fill yourself with a beautiful experience. How do you look? Is your face radiating? Are your eyes smiling? What are you wearing? What is your posture like? Is your back straight, your chin high; are your gestures unhurried, spacious and generous? Do you feel and look expanded? Does it feel good being you?

Now check yourself at your worst. How do you look when tired, fearful or angry? What is your face like? What about your posture? Are you emotionally and physically shrinking? You can use the difference in the two images to better comprehend your emotional state. This will look different for each person. I notice what makes me expand—people, activities and things I genuinely love and enjoy. These are healthy for me and I capitalize on them. The people, activities and things that make me shrink are what I need to get over or temporarily avoid until I learn how to better cope with them.

---

# The body knows better

The opposite of ease is dis-ease. When annoyance, fear or pain build up, they won't go away simply by us ignoring them. Instead, we have three options:

1. Suppress them

2. Take them out on somebody else

3. Dissolve them purposefully and safely

By suppressing them, we keep their energy trapped inside us. It may then transform to life blocks, obstructing our happiness, or it will be used up by the body in self-destructive ways, causing discomfort. When stress signals are consistently ignored, they gradually enlarge, demanding our attention in a painful way. A disease may then develop.

The body knows everything it needs to know for its wellbeing. It knows what is natural and what is forced. The mind often stands in the way of this awareness. It thinks it knows everything when in fact it is obstructing our communication with the body. If we learn to shut the mind up for a while, we can listen to the body.

When the school gymnast was instructing us how to march in a particular way for official school ceremonies, half of us got it wrong. What was natural and effortless—walking—became the product of thinking and effort. While we could walk well all day long, when marching at the rehearsals, we got confused from overthinking it. The mind wasn't helpful. By unwinding and allowing the body to do what it naturally does, we got it right.

Equally, the body knows when it is time to release trapped, destructive energy. Pressure vessels, used in hydraulics, are closed containers in which energy builds up in the absence of an escape route that would allow the pressure to vent.[39] They can be extremely dangerous. As the pressure rises above a critical value, the slightest weakness or material failure can cause violent rupture and an implosion or explosion. A safety valve must always be fitted to prevent this. Human bodies behave in a similar way. When pressure builds up inside with no opportunity to vent, there is significant risk of collapse. Externalizing emotional pressure is evidence of the body's intelligence.

The body depressurizes by releasing stored energy. Its natural depressurizing mechanisms include yawning,[40] sighing[41] and crying.[42] We think that crying is a sign of weakness. It is not. It is confirmation of our evolution. Weeping is a relief valve. Vomiting sometimes works in a similar way. The stomach naturally expels content it cannot process: be it food or emotions it cannot digest. When a friend lost his father in a car accident, for six months he woke up every morning feeling sick. He threw up and was fine for the rest of the day. That was his body's way of decompressing and dissipating the painful energy he felt.

When emotions push for a way out, I want to externalize them in healthy ways that don't harm myself or others. Even when I have the urge to act out, I know that my impulse has nothing to do with another person—it is my need to channel energy out of my body. Deliberate release mechanisms include physical exercise, purposeful muscle relaxation, conscious release of low-energy frequencies and specific breathing practices.[43]

Some of my friends have taken up boxing to dissipate energy after a stressful day. Yelling works too. Instead of yelling at people, yelling at no one helps release energy without hurting others or getting into misunderstandings. In yoga, there is a pose called Lion Pose (*Simhasana* in Sanskrit). In this exercise, the yogi imitates the lion's roar. The pose is often used for stress and anger management, as it helps release energy safely in a caring environment.

# It smells like mayday

My body reacts physically to stressors to warn me of danger. What seem to be troublesome sensitivities are in fact natural protection mechanisms. My body knows extreme conditions—external and internal—are potentially life-threatening and tries to alert me. More finely tuned than my digestive or circulatory systems, my nervous system is my personal emergency alarm.

Stressors come in many forms. They may relate to my surroundings (external) or my emotions (internal). I have a low tolerance to temperature extremes. Intense summer heat, too much exposure to direct sunlight, freezing temperatures or extreme humidity are likely to give me physical symptoms. Intense worry, sadness, anger and fake laughter sometimes have the same effect. I clench my jaw and fists, the muscles in my neck and shoulders tense and, if I don't relax, I may get a migraine. When I smell petrol or gas, my nose picks up a signal: the presence of a harmful chemical substance. My cognitive mechanism translates this to danger and my body's alarm goes off: "*Mayday! Mayday!* There is a hazardous substance over here. Get out!"

Unless I swiftly remove myself from the threat, I will probably get a headache or nausea: anything that will *make* me move away. The more life-threatening the stressor, the more pronounced the effect. Knowing how my body works doesn't alleviate the pain, but it helps me make sense of what is happening. As well as teaching myself to be more resilient, I can—in the meantime—protect myself from difficult stressors. If I can't avoid them, I can at least minimize my exposure.

The body's delicate warning mechanism picks up all sorts of signals, hazards to do with sound, smell, touch, taste and vision, as well as people's intentions. When someone is lying, hiding something from me or trying to mislead me, my throat muscles constrict and my breathing becomes shallow. Even though my mind doesn't yet know what is wrong, my body is aware that something is off and gives me a heads up. Every time I doubt, question or second-guess these warnings, I regret it. It turns out that the mechanism is infallible.

---

### EXPERIMENT 4: NOTICING THE SENSES

Throughout the day, our senses continuously pick up signals carrying important data, but we sometimes don't know how to decode them. Observe any subtle physical changes in your body and question the message they are trying to communicate. Spend a few moments noticing smells in your environment and ask yourself: "What information do they transmit? Is it safe to be here?" Pay attention to goosebumps, changes in your heartbeat, flushes or gut feelings that show up as slight shifts in your physical state. What are they telling you? Is there a threat? Is there excitement? Observe if your mouth waters or feels dry. Is there expectation or desire? Stress, worry, anxiety? Detect any pseudo coughing. Is your body trying to get rid of something—physical or emotional?

Dedicate a week to noticing your senses. Be curious about where they are taking you. Listen to your gut instinct and use it to make decisions of low significance. At lunchtime consider: "What would be a healthy and nutritious lunch for me today?" Trust the answer and choose accordingly. If the answer consistently points you to junk or otherwise unhealthy food, question the need behind it. Is it scarcity? Loss? Lack of tenderness and comfort? You can then release this and proceed.

---

# Undesirable life patterns

Sometimes my body doesn't react to stressors and self-imposed limitations, but something else does: life. Incapacitating emotions and beliefs prevent the good things from showing up. If I am afraid of failure, I either fail or I never try. If I constantly dread getting hurt, I become hurt or I self-isolate. If I desperately try to avoid people of a particular personality, I keep getting involved with such persons.

Undesirable life patterns appear when a need wants to be addressed or a wound to be healed. If I keep attracting needy people, I look at what part of me is inviting them: perhaps it is my unconscious tendency to care for people who feel neglected. Caring for people is wonderful, as long as it is done consciously. It's a lot healthier to volunteer and contribute to a cause than to unconsciously attract people who mistake me for their mother and are anxiously attached to me.

According to the principle of causality, there is a cause-and-effect relationship to everything that happens—but which is which?[44] Which is the cause, which is the effect and how do they relate? Sometimes this is not easy to discern because cause and effect keep re-occurring, creating a loop, and it becomes difficult to recognize the root cause.

If my poor self-worth and low self-esteem lead me to believe I am unlovable, chances are I don't have many people who love me in my life. This may look like confirmation that I am indeed unlovable: because I am unlovable (cause), nobody loves me (effect). I give up on myself and things get worse.

There is another possible explanation. At some point in my life, possibly as a child, I was deprived of love. This shaped the subconscious belief that I am unlovable, flawed and undeserving, and because I *believe* I am unlovable (cause), I don't allow people to express their love to me (effect). Perhaps I drive them away by being needy, insecure, defensive, aloof. Maybe I don't attract people who *can* love me because I subconsciously think I am undeserving.

If I combine these two, I realize that a shocking or traumatic past experience, or a difficult childhood, may be the reason (cause) I push away people who could love me, and attract those who are emotionally unavailable (effect). My failed relationships have nothing to do with my worth. They are the result of a past, long-forgotten yet unresolved experience. To overcome this pattern of hurtful, failing relationships, I need to surface the past and work toward healing it.

We have all been broken and we can all mend. My past doesn't have to determine my present or future. To disengage from the past, I pay attention to areas of my life that I don't like. Somewhere, I hold a belief that prevents me from unfolding a specific part of myself. Every time I find and expose such a rigid conviction, a slight fissure is created on this belief's solid crust. I can then fill that tiny cleft with self-love, light and compassion, crack it open and dissolve the debilitating belief. I can see myself as whole again. When life sucks, there is an opportunity to learn, heal, upgrade, grow stronger and wiser.

## Telltale emotions

Nobody wants to feel bad. It's exhausting. When low feelings show up seemingly uninvited, it is because they want to be heard. Rejecting them is a short-term measure. They insist and persist. They are guests in my life and they demand attention. In many ancient civilizations, mistreating guests was considered an insult, an offense, a sin.[45] God(s) protected guests and even when there was animosity between states, families or individuals, it was the host's sacred duty to treat their guests respectfully and generously. A traveler arriving at someone's doorstep was thought to be God-sent. There was a reason God(s), or fate, led them there: they brought news or they acted as a catalyst for change. Perhaps they came to redeem a debt, bring closure, make peace or re-establish balance. Emotions are the same. We don't like all of them—as we don't always like our guests—but they all have a reason for visiting.

Like guests, emotions are transient. They come and go. Even if we dislike their company, we can trust they will eventually go away. We can tolerate them, use them to gain insights or obtain information, even befriend them. I have a trick-or-treat relationship with my emotional guests. Unless I treat them, they keep returning, tricking me, until they get what they want: to pass on their message. To treat them means to invite them in and hear them out; to be courteous, polite and respectful. After all, they are just messengers and shooting the messenger is pointless. I can be sympathetic, gentle and comforting. They are here for *my* sake. I don't have to let them stay if I don't want to. I can listen to their story and I can tell them mine. We can exchange news, share information and close pending business. I can then graciously send them on their way. Departing acknowledged and content, they are unlikely to come back.

It is to my benefit to use telltale emotions cleverly, treating them as allies rather than dismissing them as enemies. I can use them to establish inner peace without ever going to war.

## The gift of pain

Our physiology and our psychology are interwoven. The body expresses what the soul feels.

If I need treatment from doctors, I follow their instructions, take the prescribed medication and do my best to take care of myself physically, mentally and spiritually. The least I can do is slow down, clear my mind from fears, worries and concerns, and treat myself with what makes me happy. I acknowledge that, at least to an extent, illnesses of the body reflect wounds of the soul. Therefore, to have lasting healing, along with helping my body recover, I also need to work on curing the soul. Otherwise, the health problem will probably re-occur or another one will show up. I need to address the root cause of my dis-comfort or dis-ease and ask myself: "What is bothering me? What is making me sick? What don't I tolerate? What can't I digest? What do I need to let go of?"

Energy healers associate each area of the body with a specific emotion or emotional quality. A malfunctioning organ or a painful body part guides them to identify the emotional state which may be the root cause of a problem. Although this is neither scientifically proven nor consistent with all people, these associations are often accurate. They make a useful starting point to identify the emotion(s) underlying a physical condition. The following are just examples:

- Clenching the jaw, making a fist or locking joints is the result of tension or fear stored in the body. The fight, flight or freeze mechanism kicks in and the body instantly prepares for combat. This may be accompanied by an urge to empty the bladder. The body seeks to settle all pending business so that it can entirely focus on the imminent danger.

- Discomfort in the throat often signifies reluctance in expressing emotions, needs or desires, difficulty in communicating, or suppressed feelings. This happens to me when I am upset or hurt and I keep it to myself.

- Stomachache may be linked to fear and loss of courage. I sometimes feel nausea when I am overwhelmed and want to give up.

- Pain in the lower abdomen may be related to blocked creativity.

- Back issues can be insecurity or lack of support. It is as though nobody has my back and I am exposed.

- Trouble with legs and feet is often associated with fear of moving forward, lack of confidence or indecision.

- Skin irritations may be connected to toxicity that the body wants to expel. When this happens, I know I have toxic emotions stuck inside that need to be released.

- Tinnitus may be my response to overstimulation. The body is saying: "I don't want to hear. I don't want to know. I need a break. Leave me alone." I experience this when I can't take any more stress and worry. I want my senses to shut down.

- Ancient civilizations considered the liver the seat of human emotions.[46] Its malfunctioning was associated with suppressed feelings and unexpressed creativity.

- The thymus (the gland protected by the collarbone) is believed to be responsible for the optimal operation of the immune system.[47]

- When the desires of the mind and those of the heart are in conflict, it is usually the neck that becomes painful. The neck is the bridge between head and heart, mind and soul, and when heart and mind are misaligned, the neck is in distress. It's easy to know what the mind wants because it keeps reminding me. It doesn't let me forget. The heart, however, speaks more subtly and it is harder for me to find out what she needs. As a result, she may be silently suffering. My neck also hurts when I feel overly responsible for people other than myself. Assuming responsibility for others is not healthy. It literally weighs me down. My neck aches as though a load is hanging from it.

In my late twenties, I unexpectedly developed hay fever, caused by olive tree blossoms. For the next fifteen years, I suffered every spring. There was no apparent explanation for my body's reaction to the awakening of nature. I used to live in a place abundant in olive trees, which made April and May problematic. *Ignoring* the allergy wouldn't trick it away. When I realized that these physical symptoms were a manifestation of my emotional state, I set about healing my sadness and sorrow, and the symptoms reduced and gradually went away.

Many healers concur that the left side of our body is mainly related to our feminine side, and the right to our masculine side. Health issues arising consistently on one side of the body may indicate that either our masculinity or femininity is suppressed or misused. The left side could also indicate *internal* struggles, while the right side is associated with *external* triggers. A distressing thought may show up in the form of discomfort in the left side of the body, whereas overexposure to an irritating external stimulus may give rise to soreness on the right side.

Even though I have repeatedly experienced many of these symptoms, I can't take the explanations above for granted. Every time discomfort occurs, I need to dialogue with my body to find out what is going on. When I feel sick, I trust the first emotion or picture that comes to mind as soon as the physical symptoms show up, as this is usually the root cause of their occurrence. Pain is difficult to accept, but it can be a gift if I use it to point me in the direction of caring for myself by considering: "What is asking for my attention? What needs to be released? What wants to be healed?"

## Summary

- We can use our body as a compass, as most physical body symptoms point to an emotional state.

- In Experiment 3 we learn what our expanded and contracted self looks like.

- Our body knows when it needs to release trapped energy. We can follow up on the body's request and release emotions in safe ways.

- Our bodies have emergency alerting mechanisms in place to warn us of danger. These often show up as physical symptoms.

- In Experiment 4 we practice noticing the senses, including the gut, and the messages they convey.

- Suppressed emotions or limiting beliefs may lead to undesirable life patterns.

- Unpleasant emotions may be uncomfortable, but they are useful because they communicate messages about our beliefs and level of perception.

- Pain can be used as a source of information regarding which aspects of ourselves need attention and emotional healing.

# 21

# Vibrating

A lbert Einstein's theory of special relativity includes the famous equation that relates energy and mass:

$$E = mc^2$$

where E = energy in joules (J), m = mass in kilograms (kg), and c = the speed of light in meters per second $(3 \times 10^8 \text{ m/s})$[48]

Scientists have proved what ancient mystics intuitively knew: everything is energy. Matter is nothing more than slow-moving energy. *We* are energy. When I multiply my mass by the speed of light squared, I can calculate the energy I am composed of. It's an impressive figure. We are colossal energy.

Living beings and nonliving things are made up of molecules and atoms vibrating at specific frequencies.[49] In humans, these frequencies vary depending on our mood, emotions, thoughts and intentions, as well as our subconscious beliefs. The vibrations we emit affect our surroundings. They are received by other beings and things, mostly in our vicinity. Along with all other living creatures, we are transducers: we simultaneously send and receive vibrations.

What we sometimes sense about a person or place is the quality of transmitted or lingering energy. Light, bright energy feels happy, gentle, encouraging, rejuvenating, safe and loving. Even though we may not be explicitly aware of it, we feel good when absorbing these high vibrations from our environment. We rarely question this because we are happy and content. Dense, heavy energy feels uncomfortable, suspicious, aggressive, hostile, tiring and frightening. We feel off-balance when we receive low vibrations. This bothers us, but we may not know the reason.

Since everything is energy, when it comes to experiencing and perceiving life, our energy *sensors*—our senses—are more important than we think. Sensing vibrations is what our bodies are designed to do. We may sense heaviness as a fast or irregular heartbeat, a weight on the chest, a lump in the throat, a stomachache, heavy legs, weak knees, tense muscles, sweating or being short of breath. We sense lightness as heart or chest expansion and muscle relaxation. When the body feels healthy and happy, breathing is relaxed, deep, steady and unobstructed, the heart rate is stable and the stomach is calm.

Information is abundant in the Universe and manifests as a *formation*:[50] it takes on a form to be transported, transferred and communicated. Vibrations carry information, just like soundwaves carry a voice or music. We continuously receive inaudible energy waves, but our ability to interpret them accurately is limited. Asking questions, *sensing* the answer and then putting it into context based on the principle of cause and effect is a sensible way to perceive the world. Our senses have their own vocabulary. Learning it improves our ability to decipher vibes when they show up. There is a reason we associate unpleasant emotions with low-frequency energy and pleasant ones with high frequencies. From Einstein's relativity equation, we deduct that the higher the energy, the more mass it can create. It is easier for higher energy to create matter. Higher energy has more creative power.

Another equation from the discipline of quantum physics, formulated by Max Planck, relates energy to frequency:

$$E = hv$$

where E = energy in joule (J), h = Planck's Universal constant, v = frequency in Hz[51]

Higher frequencies carry more energy. If we substitute energy (E) in Einstein's equation with Planck's energy-frequency relationship (E = hv), we get the relationship:

$$hv = mc^2$$

137

The creation of matter (m) is proportional to frequency (v). The higher the frequency, the higher the creating ability.

When we are happy and loving, vibrating in the high range of frequencies, we feel light and energized and we create. When we are angry and fearful, vibrating in the low-frequency range, we feel heavy, de-energized, uncreative and unproductive. We may even tend to destroy. Love, one of the topmost vibrational frequencies, is the force driving the birth of our offspring, the most miraculous of human creations. Fear, toward the bottom of the vibrational range, causes war, destruction and death. The Map of Consciousness is aligned with this deduction.[52]

---

### EXPERIMENT 5: FEELING THE VIBE

Sit quietly and close your eyes. Think of something that makes you happy and increase the thought in magnitude as much as you can. Notice the sensation in your body. How each body responds to a certain vibrational frequency is unique. For me, happiness is usually associated with warmth in the chest and expansion of the heart.

Now, bring a sad, upsetting or fearful thought to mind. Notice how *this* feels in your body. For me, fear shows up as discomfort in the stomach—I literally feel a punch in the gut—or my muscles get stiff: I clench my jaw, fists or shoulders. Sadness feels like a lump stuck in my throat.

Try this with two groups of emotions:

- Guilt
- Remorse
- Shame
- Blame
- Obsession
- Failure
- Insecurity
- Self-doubt
- Fear

- Friendliness
- Compassion
- Humor
- Joy
- Passion
- Freedom
- Peace
- Confidence
- Love

The group on the left are fear-based emotions; the group on the right are love-based sentiments. My body responds distinctly differently to each of these two groups. When I experience physical discomfort for no apparent reason, I check if I can link it to an underlying emotion. Is it love- or fear-based? This way, I can translate what my body feels into an emotional state. If I can find a pattern, there is probably a close relationship between the two.

Observe yourself for a few days or weeks before drawing conclusions about your body's unique vocabulary. Bear in mind that this may change at some point.

---

# I feel for you

Empathy is the sensitivity to picking up energy waves emitted by others and the ability of one person to sense what another feels.[53] Most of us sympathize with others when they feel low. We *know* how they feel and are sad for them and with them. Some of us, however, literally *sense* another person's physical discomfort, pain or emotional state in our own bodies. I get empathic symptoms without consciously knowing that another person is going through a particular experience. Dialing a person's phone number, I sometimes know how they feel before they pick up. Perhaps they are sad, anxious, excited or happy; maybe their heartbeat is fast, or their breath is deep and regular: I feel these symptoms in my body. This is how I often intuitively know someone is in trouble.

Empathy is sometimes mistaken for hypochondria and vice versa. Hypochondria is a fear-based condition. I become a hypochondriac when, knowing that another person is ill or in pain, I become hyper aware of my own body. Due to anxiety, I may then unconsciously replicate the same physical distress. What if I have the same illness? However, hypochondria is driven by worry and obsession over our own health, whereas empathy is love-based. It is powered by our concern for another individual. When I am in empathic pain, I am not anxious about *my* health and what will happen to *me*. I can tell that the discomfort isn't mine.

Highly empathic individuals often get affected by the overlapping energies of people in their proximity. I would rather have a couple of people repainting my house, even if it takes them longer, than a big crew working in my house for only a few days. It is easier for me to manage the energies of two to three people than to accommodate the energies of so many strangers at once.

# A blessing or a curse?

Empaths are in the middle of a scale of consciousness. On one end are individuals who are not inclined toward helping others. These people have fewer and weaker empathic experiences. They shut down their sensory ability to receive other people's energy waves. They remain impervious to another person's pain, as well as to another's joy. They are less concerned about shared problems but also share less happiness. On the other extreme are those with significantly heightened perception, who are fully aware of what is going on around them without feeling it physically. This is due to their ability to decode the energy they receive *before* it manifests as a physical symptom in their own body. They interpret the necessary information at the level of consciousness instead of the physical level. This way, they can skip the painful stage and work out directly what the problem is.

Empaths receive a signal, but can only perceive the information it carries by physically experiencing the sensation. In a world of struggles and worries, empathy brings us closer. It enables us to get into someone else's shoes and share their experience. It increases our tolerance and compassion. It helps us forgive because not only do we *know* how the other person feels, we can also *feel* it. As empaths, we easily absorb people's happiness as well as their pain. We can be sincerely happy for another person's success, and we have more reasons to be happy ourselves, more often. Nevertheless, empathy is not the most comfortable sensation.

When people around us are confused, upset or suffering, it can be overwhelming, painful and depleting.

Empathy may be a characteristic of those of us who want to be helpful but don't know how. When one of my children has a stomachache, I often get one too. This is because, at a subconscious level, I would rather *I* had the problem instead of them. As a result, we both end up in pain. Empathy helps in *understanding* but not in *alleviating* suffering. This is not practically useful. The overall pain experienced is doubled.

What is it that still makes me so eager to absorb another person's distress? My best guess is that I willingly take up people's pain to help them dissolve it; but if I don't know how, I get stuck with it—at least temporarily. When this happens, I can no longer ignore it. It hurts and I need to do something about it. The best I can do is to consciously work on dissolving the uncomfortable energy. Then the other person starts feeling better and so do I.

It is often hard to be an empath. I sometimes wish my empathy would go away and leave me alone. Deep down, though, I know it is not without benefits. I have empathy to thank for my capacity to love, forgive and care for others. We empaths can sense the *intention* behind a person's behavior no matter how hard they try to disguise it. Even when faces are smiling and words are polite, the energy people emit gives them away. This makes us vigilant in negotiations and hard to manipulate. Instead of getting rid of empathy, I am working on getting over the stage of physical suffering by enhancing my perception, awareness and consciousness. I remind myself that I am not supposed to carry the weight of others in my body all the time. We each forge our life paths and can only bear responsibility for ourselves. We can help each other out, but we don't have to suffer along with everyone who is suffering.

## Summary

- We are made up of vibrating molecules and atoms. The higher our vibrating frequencies, the higher our feel-good emotions and the better our ability to create.

- In Experiment 5 we experiment with sensing how various emotions are expressed in our bodies so that we can match physical sensations to emotional states.

- Empathy is our ability to sense another person's physical or emotional distress in our own bodies.

- Empathy brings people closer and gives us an opportunity to help, but it doesn't have to be destructive to our own wellbeing.

# 22

# Reconsidering Our Place In The World

We sometimes find consolation in thinking that others are worse off than us, but this is incompatible with a fundamental principle: as elements (or subsystems) of the same system—our Universe—all forms of life are connected. We are all interrelated in that each one of us is an integral part of humanity, nature, Earth, the Universe and the Cosmos. Forgetting this, I may believe I am unaffected by that horrible story on the news as long as it is not happening to me. However, even though I may not be able to perceive this, whatever happens out there has an impact on me.

The cell analogy helps us to comprehend this better. Over 37 trillion cells make up a functioning human body.[54] We can think of them as a community of cells, workers in the human factory, each of which is an autonomous microorganism with its own intelligence,[55] specialization, life cycle and health record. Each has a mission, a role, a plan, a capacity. It uses input to produce output. It has its own command centers, life expectancy and regeneration abilities. Some cells fall ill; others stay healthy; some age faster than others—exactly as in a community of humans. Being elements of the same system does not prevent us from also being self-governing: deciding for ourselves and making conscious, personal choices.

We know that cells are interdependent parts of a larger whole because we can see that particular whole: the body of a living being. We are larger than a cell and can easily see the bigger picture. A cell may not be able to comprehend this. It is too small to zoom out and take a look at the body of which it is a tiny part. In its ignorance, the cell may not care about the body's wellbeing or the welfare of its fellow cells. The cell has limited perception of the scale of the reality in which it belongs. It lives in its microcosm, oblivious to how it contributes to the human body as a larger system. We, however, know that as tiny as a cell may be, it is vital and indispensable to the body. It has its place, function, importance and contribution. Without it, the human body system wouldn't be as it is. Fortunately, our autonomous cells co-operate.

We often miss the fact that—like a cell—we are parts of an extended holon, a unit larger than us. We don't see the bigger picture because, while it is relatively easy to conceive what is smaller than ourselves, it is difficult to comprehend systems larger than us as coherent units. We can break down a living organism into organs, cells, molecules, atoms, electrons, quarks, etc. It is difficult to conceive what we are the breakdown *of*. Since we are *part* of it and *in* it, we can't get out of it and observe it from a distance. If we could somehow have a bird's eye view of what lies outside of us, at a macroscopic scale, it would be easier to conceive that humanity is one living organism.

Everything has an impact on us, but we can consciously choose what to do with it: observe, learn, heal and proceed; or limit ourselves by adopting a disempowering belief. At the same time, we have an impact on everything and everyone else, and we can choose the quality of this impact: are we filling the world with love or are we stuffing it with fear?

Scientists of many disciplines are currently working together to reveal the bigger picture, identify our place in it and comprehend our interdependencies. They are getting closer. Even without scientific proof, philosophers, meditators and shamans across many cultures and civilizations have had and are having glimpses of this big picture. Expanded perception enables us to approach this experience of being part of a whole.

## Collective consciousness and God's mind

Most scientists agree that our Universe started as a point of immense concentrated energy. I visualize this 13.8 billion-year-old source of energy of Lilliputian proportions as a bright dot in the darkness.[56]

The energy within this dot is condensed within a confined space and has nowhere to go; it does not disperse. It contains *everything*: all there is to know about our Universe and its inhabitants, all the energy required to create and sustain them, the instructions for living. It is all-encompassing, and so powerful that it can generate life. It has created us and everything around us.

At some point our Universe began expanding and still is. The initiation of its expansion is what we refer to as the Big Bang.[57] I imagine the expansion of the Universe as an inflating balloon. When my children were little, we used to host their birthday parties at home. To keep the kids occupied, I would take a set of new balloons and use a thin marker to write words and numbers or make simple sketches on them. I then inflated them. As the balloon inflated, the inscriptions on its surface were enlarged and distorted, and their color faded. The distance between numbers, letters and words increased and it became more difficult for the kids to work out what I had scribbled. We played all sorts of games using balloons to read messages, guess colors or find patterns and hidden symbols in a maze of numbers, letters and signs. It wasn't easy. Drawings were misshapen, colors lost vigor and the kids often missed, duplicated or lost count of symbols. As the balloon inflated, the information on its surface was not lost, but it spread and faded. It became harder to find.

As the Universe expands, the same amount of energy and information that was once contained in that dot is scattered in a vast volume of three-dimensional space (or area of a possibly two-dimensional Universe[58]). The observable part of our Universe alone has a diameter of about $10^{26}$ m.[59] That original energy and information is now playing hide-and-seek in every corner of this space. Information keeps dispersing and it becomes increasingly difficult to put the pieces of the puzzle together. As we professionally specialize to drill deeper into knowledge, it is more critical than ever that we work together if we are not to lose sight of the holon, the system of which we are parts.

Many people believe in the power of joint prayer, as collective willpower partly counterbalances the dispersion of energy. It is more potent than isolated individual intentionality because it reconcentrates the energy, power and will that has become scattered. Collective consciousness approaches that initial condensed energy and power of the Universe in its original point form. Collective prayer brings together thousands or even millions of personal yearnings into a single resolve. This can create a tremendous concentration of energy and is a powerful momentum for change.

If we could put together the knowledge of all people who live, have lived and will live in the Universe, not only would we have a more complete set of information, but from that, we would be able to draw further conclusions. Universal mind is the collective consciousness of all conscious beings in our Universe, including humans. It is all our minds together.

Most scientists believe that our Universe is finite[60] and is not the only universe in the Cosmos. This suggests the existence of an even greater source of energy and intelligence outside our Universe and bigger than it. It is from this source that our Universe was born. This energy source is what spiritual leaders call God, God's mind, cosmic mind or cosmic consciousness. It is the collective consciousness contained in all universes, plus the initial spark that ignited it. When I want assistance, guidance, awareness and support, I reach out to this source of inconceivable energy. I request that, as a part of it, as its offspring, I can access some of this unlimited wisdom, clarity, strength, love and creativity.

---

### EXPERIMENT 6:
### THE EXTENDED-FAMILY MEDITATION

Sitting in a relaxed position, eyes closed, breathing deeply, bring your attention to your heart. Picture it as a small flower bursting open, emitting love and warmth. Take a few moments to feel this wave of warmth and allow it to ripple outward. With every breath, feel this surge of warmth expanding until it wraps your body and the space around you. Submerge yourself in the love and trust it represents. Allow yourself to feel safe, empowered and cared for. Imagine the ripples of warmth expanding further until they cover everything and everyone on the globe, like a soft, comfy blanket of love. Mentally remind yourself that all people are your brothers and sisters, mothers and fathers, sons and daughters. Extend your love toward them. Wish them to be safe, healthy and happy.

Through this meditation, I expand my consciousness and consider all people my family. It has allowed me to re-establish my relationship with people and the world and feel, for any person, the same level of compassion and tenderness I instinctively show my children, partner, parents and close friends.

Considering everyone as family doesn't make me a pushover, a victim or a stepping stone. I can still take care of myself. I protect myself from conduct and contact that has a negative impact on me. I avoid or minimize my exposure to people and activities that drain me. The difference is that I no longer have hard feelings toward the people I avoid. Minimizing interaction with them is not punishing or disliking them. It is keeping myself peaceful and calm. It is about me, not them. This way, I stay clear of resentment, as I no longer blame them for my anger, sadness or depletion.

## Zooming in and out

When I zoom out of me, I can see where I belong, the bigger picture. I recognize that my cat Boris and I, even though we belong to different species, are partners sharing the same ecosystem. If I can share a house with my immediate family, I can also share the Planet with my extended family—Boris and all other earthly creatures—co-operatively. We are all Earth's stakeholders and it's in our best interests to keep our Planet and one another healthy and prosperous. Zooming out, my problems look trivial. Having an appointment canceled at the last minute may be upsetting, but it doesn't have to be. On a larger scale, it seems as important as Boris chasing his tail. Whenever my day is challenging, I zoom out and everything looks more manageable.

More than 8 billion hominins inhabit the Earth right now,[61] living their stories in parallel. Zooming in on this vast set of people, I realize that every individual has their stories, their highs and lows, their successes and failures. I know nothing about them, but I am sure all they want is to be happy. I don't know what happiness means to them and how they are making it happen. What I *do* know is that—even though it doesn't always look like it—they are doing their best, just as I am. They have an impact on their family and their community. Sometimes they make people laugh and sometimes they are cranky. Each one matters to a small group of people who make a difference to a larger group, who in turn affect a bigger one. This is where we indirectly meet.

When people around me are pushing through their lives, sometimes being rude, inconsiderate or hurtful, I zoom in. Looking at them from the outside in, I recognize that they too have their troubles. Their problems and struggles may be irrelevant to me, but they are important to *them*. Their awful temper has nothing to do with me. They are having a bad day, just as I sometimes do. I can be patient and respectful, which is what *I* require of others when I'm not having a good day.

# Summary

- Each person is part of humanity, just like a cell is part of a human body. We are both autonomous and interdependent.

- Collective consciousness is the awareness of all living beings in the Cosmos, and we are part of it.

- In Experiment 6 we extend our love towards all earthly beings and things.

- Zooming in and out of ourselves helps us better comprehend the world.

# 23
# Healing

If not now, when? Will there ever be an ideal time to allow myself to express genuinely? There will always be unfinished business to attend to, people to care for, work to be done, obstacles to be overcome, problems to be solved, excuses. Now is as good a time as any to take action.

It is one thing knowing what to do and another thing doing it. Sometimes I know exactly what I *need* to do, but I don't know *how*. At other times, I know how but I still don't do it. Indecision, habit and inertia hold me back. Taking action is a choice. It doesn't happen on its own. It requires intention and effort. It involves letting go of disempowering beliefs but also leaving my comfort zone. Sometimes it means being willing to lose something to gain something else. It entails taking risks. Nothing is guaranteed.

For the releasing process to be effective, it is imperative to:

- Acknowledge that *there is* a problem or limitation

- Identify it

- Be willing to rectify it, learn the associated lesson and apply it

- Believe that it is possible

Unless we *believe* that change can happen, it is unlikely it will because we are slamming the door to it. The least we can do is remain neutral, curious and open to possibilities, willing to be surprised.

## Surrendering to vulnerability

The word "surrender" rings of impotence. It is associated with resignation, giving up, succumbing, being overpowered. Is it always an act of weakness? It's easy to surrender to overeating or watching TV for hours. It requires the least effort and is temporarily comforting. Surrendering to life, the way it unfolds and how things are, is an act of courage. It is a virtue that has been sought after and cultivated for thousands of years.

We resist life's flow because, more than anything, we want to be in control. We think this is a sign of strength when it is more an indication of fear and lack of trust. Surrendering to where life is taking us requires us to make peace with uncertainty. We are not ready for this. Uncertainty breeds anxiety for the unpredictable. Where is my life going? What if I can't cope? What if I don't like it? What if I get hurt? Since we don't want to surrender, we resist. Resistance is the source of many problems, including stagnation, frustration, unhappiness, distress and disease. Struggling is energy-consuming, harmful to our health and emotionally upsetting. If we could channel our energy toward making the best of what comes along the way, we would be more efficient, effective, peaceful and happier.

Surrendering to life requires accepting our vulnerability.[62] It means acknowledging that we cannot control everything around us and are not supposed to. Sometimes we have it our way and sometimes we don't. One day we win; the next day we lose. Even though we know this, surrendering to it takes courage. It takes courage to willingly let go of our fierce need for control without giving up. The word "courage" comes from the French *cœur*, which means heart. True power arises from the heart, not the mind. It is not a result of willfulness or the application of force, but a product of love and compassion. Self-compassion spares us pointless struggles and disappointment. Loving life, nature and its creatures, we have less to fight against.

Surrendering to vulnerability is liberating. It shifts me from survival to thriving mode, from struggle to flow. Accepting life as it is does not mean that I stop seeking change; that I stay passive and inactive. It means doing my best with what I have without grumbling. I am focusing on the solution instead of the problem, skipping the drama stage.

How do I surrender? I stop complaining and resisting. I embrace my imperfections. Being uniquely imperfect makes life fun, interesting and less stressful. Success and failure are interchangeable and constitute integral parts of the discovery process. When I own my failures as much as I own my successes, the failures become less dreadful and the successes more enjoyable.

---

### EXPERIMENT 7: RELEASING HEAVY EMOTIONS AND LIMITING BELIEFS

Releasing debilitating emotions and beliefs is a powerful healing practice. Sit comfortably. Select a belief, a pattern, a past experience or situation that bothers you: fear of failure, procrastination, low self-esteem, a regretful decision, a shocking incident. Allow the associated feeling to come up. What emotion does this belief, pattern or experience evoke? How does it feel in your body? Are you getting tense? Do you feel pain or distress? If the sensation is heavy, fearful, depressive or destructive or if you feel any kind of physical discomfort, you are better off without it. You want to let it go. Instead of feeling the emotion in my body, I sometimes sense it around me: as heat in front of my face or a chill behind my back. It may be in a visual or audio form or it may appear as a taste or smell. Sometimes I get goosebumps.

Take a few moments to appreciate what you have learned from this challenging experience, behavioral pattern or belief, even if it is as simple as choosing to overcome it. You may want to make a note of the learning point(s) in your diary.

Set your intention toward letting go of the emotion and sending the particular belief, pattern or experience away. Its mission has been accomplished: you have learned your lesson. It is now time to release it and permanently let it go. Take a deep breath in and fill your lungs with determination.

Love is the best antidote to fear and any other low-frequency emotion. Inhaling and exhaling deeply and slowly, feel a strong surge of love rising from your heart, expanding in your chest. Inhale and exhale, flushing the part of your body that is in distress with self-love. The low-frequency emotion is dissolved under this almighty pure love. Your vibrating frequency elevates to the ranges of love, joy and peace.

Sit quietly for a moment. Check how your body feels. If the discomfort reduces or shifts to another part of the body, repeat the experiment until your body feels neutral or light. If the discomfort persists, allow a few days to pass and repeat the process. Clearing will continue subconsciously in the meantime.

---

# The onion effect

Asking questions allows me to solve trivial as well as complex problems: what to cook for dinner, how to break bad news to someone, how to work out what is holding me back from the things I love. As I practice this, certain things happen:

- I become more mindful. My mind is more practical, less preoccupied with endless theories and useless excuses. I can stay present in the moment for longer.

- My questioning skills improve and questions become more targeted. Answers flow more freely, quickly and accurately.

- My creativity, efficiency and effectiveness increase.

- Worries and time spent on worrying decrease.

- Deeper concerns are uncovered.

As I probe, I peel off a layer of conceptual or emotional constraints and there is a chance that another, deeper insecurity or incapacitating conviction will be revealed. When this happens, I sometimes feel that I have woken up a dormant giant, and I wonder why I stirred things up. Facing our deepest insecurities isn't easy. At that moment, I may regret letting the genie out of the bottle, as I can no longer contain it. I have scratched the surface, and raw flesh has been exposed. There is nothing I can do other than heal it. It sometimes looks scary, but in the long run, lifting off the heaviness and releasing the junk I carry is a blessing. The benefits are so profound they wipe away all doubts. It is an investment that pays off.

We can only see the tip of an iceberg. Roughly 90% of a free-floating iceberg is submerged beneath the water surface.[63] Because it isn't visible, we may underestimate its size. We are no different. Only a small part of us is evident to others; there is a lot more hidden underneath. The problem is that the unknown part of us is also out of our *own* sight. We are often oblivious to the layers of misperceptions, disabling beliefs, dramas and traumas concealed under the facade of what we call our personality. It is unrealistic to expect that I can uncover the entire iceberg at once. I am not fit to cope with such huge revelations in one go. Exposing the iceberg is a step-by-step process that some people call spiritual evolution. It can be a lifelong experience. It starts right here, right now, by asking questions, seeking answers and releasing what is holding me back.

Shedding a coating of misconceptions, I effectively make room for the next level to come up to the surface. It is like peeling an onion. As one layer is peeled off, another one is revealed. The freshly exposed layer is tenderer as it is located closer to the core and it has never seen the light of day. It needs gentler handling. I am probably less familiar with it because it has been deeply buried for so long. I may need time to recognize and accept it. The good news is that once I start, I create momentum. My soul sees an opportunity to be heard and healed. One revelation leads to another. Peeling off the layers is an emotionally intense experience that often makes me cry—but it is part of the process. I know I have reached the core when I am left with only forgiveness and peace.

In the beginning, it may seem that this un-layering project will never end. However, after the first layers of junk are cleared away, I reach a sufficient level of peace. This is where I can take a deep breath. From that point onward, the process becomes less urgent, smoother and more natural. When I reach the necessary level of maturity, the next layer reveals itself and so on. In retrospect, I don't regret letting the genie loose. I only wish I had cracked the bottle open sooner.

## Cutting the cords

Is there any truth in the saying "The sins of the fathers are visited upon the children"? DNA holds our genetic code, and the science of epigenetics studies how our DNA is expressed.[64] Nearly every cell in our body has the same set of genes, yet different types of cells perform different functions. The living body is like a house full of almost identical siblings, each specializing in a different area of the household. Together, they keep the house organized, clean and functioning, but they don't all perform the same activities. The siblings share—to a large extent—the same DNA. What differs from one sibling to another is their agreed mission and their acquired training. The discipline of epigenetics is concerned with the energies or forces acting on the genetic material, influencing the genes' functionality, making cell specialization possible. Epigenetic processes instruct each body cell about which topic to major in. The cell then turns on or off individual genes as though it were closing the chemistry textbook and opening a book on economics. From the books that remain open, the cell receives specific education, training and instructions. It then performs the job it has learned: its professional specialization.

According to epigenetics, our cells are affected by environmental factors, nutrition, life experiences and our belief system. These external factors are adopted and internalized. Epigenetic adjustments can last a lifetime and may even be passed on, from generation to generation, without any gene modification. As a result, we may be carriers of guilt, remorse, blame, shame, fear and limitations inherited from our lineage of ancestors. The good news is that epigenetic changes are reversible. The DNA remains intact, but the body can be re-instructed on *how* to read the gene sequence.

To deliberately cut the cords between myself and my lineage, I first need to acknowledge that I may be experiencing self-destructive convictions and behaviors which are not mine. It is possible that someone or a group of people in my family or social environment adopted them long ago and that they were carried forward to me. I set my intention to release these limitations. Inherited convictions may need several iterations to be released. This is not surprising because their roots are deep and need a few thrusts to unroot. It is worth the effort not only because it liberates *me* from problems carried forward but also because it frees my children and the line of descendants that follow. It is the best gift I can pass on to my heirs.

Cutting cords with my ancestors doesn't mean I don't love or respect them or that I am turning my back on them. On the contrary, I am paying attention to what has been bothering them for generations. I am honoring their stories, learning from them and acknowledging their contribution to my growth. I am making a conscious choice to be an independent personality. I am shaping my own life path instead of continuing theirs. As much as I love, respect and honor my great-great-grandmother, I am me, not her. To the extent that I can, I will not continue carrying the burden of the past, let alone pass it on. I am healing past trauma for the generations to come as well as those that preceded. I am doing all of us a favor.

## The realm of the subconscious

Intense experiences and inherited beliefs are stored in the subconscious and affect my life even though I may not be aware of it. As strong as it may be, my intentionality is sometimes insufficient to help me overcome them, especially when I don't acknowledge their existence. A way to neutralize the adverse effects of such subconscious brainwashing is to find the hidden troublemaker, bring it to order and replace it with inspiring and empowering beliefs. I call this Hypno-Empowerment™. Using simple hypnosis techniques, I establish better communication with my subconscious. I can then identify a limiting conviction and overcome it more easily.

The human brain functions in a wide range of frequencies. When awake and fully alert, it mostly operates at β-frequencies, 12–35 Hz. While learning and creating, brain activity rises to the γ-frequency range, 35–100 Hz. In tranquility, it drops to 8–12 Hz, the α-frequency range. In deeper states of relaxation, such as sleep, hypnosis and meditation, it further drops to θ, 4–8 Hz, and δ, 0.5–4 Hz.[65] Additional frequencies such as ε and λ are currently being explored by scientists.[66]

As brain frequencies drop, our conscious mind becomes less active. It thinks less. Researchers suggest that we have between 6,000 and 70,000 thoughts in a day. This corresponds to at least four thoughts per minute.[67] Thinking about four different things every minute is a lot of work for the conscious mind. When we decelerate the rate of thinking, the conscious mind quietens. This presents an excellent opportunity to listen to—and communicate with—the subconscious. When thinking reduces, our inner critic is also quietened. With self-judgment out of the way, it is easier to admit our deepest concerns, fears and insecurities. Once we know what these are, we can make a conscious choice to give them up, or we can intentionally turn them around by giving a different ending to the story that has created them.

Hypnosis also works as a time machine.[68] While in a state of trance, it is possible to take a journey back in time and find the root cause of a current experience, behavior, habit or pattern. Our subconscious knows what has hurt it the most. In contrast, the conscious mind is so stubborn and willful that it conceals this information, trying to protect us from reliving a painful experience. This may be a good short-term coping mechanism, but in the long term it is healthier to let things go.

In hypnosis, I have the luxury to revisit a past traumatic experience, from the security of the present, as an observer rather than a victim. I can then conclude that the traumatic situation is no longer pertinent and I am now safe. I consciously prohibit my past from dictating my present and future. No matter what happened, I want something better for myself and I am determined to get it, starting *now*. I may use positive affirmations to remind myself that I am worthy, lovable, kind, capable of success and prosperity. Working under hypnosis is a brilliant shortcut. What could take the conscious mind years to do or undo can be achieved in a few weeks.

For thousands of years, mystics have used hypnosis to deepen and broaden their perception. Contemporary athletes use it to improve their track record, artists to create their best masterpieces, inventors to invent, scientists to discover and entrepreneurs to expand their business ventures. It may someday be taught at school, helping students overcome learning difficulties and tap into their unlimited potential. Hypnosis techniques can be used to expedite healing. In addition to conventional treatment and medication, under hypnosis we can gently but decisively instruct the body to function optimally, assisting recuperation. Each of our cells has its own intelligence and decision-making ability. By communicating with the subconscious, we can ultimately learn how to guide our cells to regenerate, recover and optimize their operation.

I used to be one of the many people who are reluctant to allow a hypnotist to tamper with their subconscious. We are suspicious. We don't know whom to trust. Hypnosis is a tool; as such, it can be used in both helpful and harmful ways. Self-hypnosis is a skill that can be learned and used effectively.[69] Taught by a competent teacher, anyone can learn how to hypnotize themselves. The technique can then be practiced and perfected along the way. The magic of hypnosis is not in achieving the extraordinary but in freeing ourselves of limitations and upgrading our lives.

## Freedom is a state of being

Throughout history, people have been striving for their freedom regardless of age, race, gender, religion, educational or financial background; but freedom from what? Freedom from slavery, inequality, injustice, oppression, suppression, dogmatism, autocracy, dictatorship; from how *others* demand us to behave, how *they* want us to be, what they decide *for* us. We want to be free to choose, to decide for ourselves and make our own mistakes. Is this enough?

The narrower my perception, the smaller my self-imposed imprisonment cell. How free am I when I constantly operate under anger, envy, stereotypes, resentment and fear? When all I see around me is animosity and conspiracy? When I hold grudges? When every time I long to take a step forward, I hit the confining walls of my limiting convictions? When I can't do what I love because I fear judgment, criticism or failure. External freedom can easily be conceived. It means escaping from whoever is trying to run my life for me. Internal freedom is not easy to recognize and—for this reason—it is harder to attain. It is the disengagement from limiting beliefs and emotions.

Thoughts and sentiments that prevent me from experiencing inner peace and inhibit my growth are real forms of imprisonment. They keep me in custody because they don't allow me to feel good about myself and the world. They sentence me to unhappiness. What remains when I set myself free from my own debilitating reactions to external stimuli is love and peace.

Freedom is a state of being that can be achieved any time, anywhere. A person free from damaging emotions and destructive tendencies can both *feel* and *be* safe in society. Such a person is well behaved because kindness is their natural way of expression, not because they need to respect or fear the law. They are benevolent by default. In this context, freedom becomes safe.

Freedom is, by definition, unconditional. It can't be dependent upon circumstances and variables. There are no ifs and buts; no terms and conditions. I am free when I willingly and wholeheartedly choose my actions and respect their consequences, and when I accept my emotions. Freeing myself from externally imposed restrictions, I may *look* happy. Liberating myself from the junk I carry and the fear within me, I can *be* happy.

# Forgiveness

My grandparents lived through a handful of wars. When I was little, I would climb onto my grandfather's lap, asking for his war stories—they were thrilling. During war, my granddad had a hard time in prison. He was tortured in many imaginative and brutal ways to force him to disclose information. What didn't make sense to me was that he never complained or blamed his tormentors. I was young and I wanted justice for him, but he didn't seem to share these emotions. When I grew older, I asked him if he hated those people. My granddad said: "No. I don't. They were doing their job and I was doing mine."

He had forgiven them.

Forgiveness is not just saying the words. It is genuinely holding no hard feelings. It cannot be forced or faked because it is not a gesture. It is energy: a state of grace, a release. I have been wronged many times throughout the years, but I have also hurt people. On some occasions, I did this unknowingly. On others, I knew exactly what I was doing and I still did it. Then I regretted it. It was a mistake. Making mistakes doesn't make me unworthy of forgiveness. I still deserve another chance and if *I* do, then *everyone* does.

To forgive, I don't have to concur that all actions and behaviors are acceptable. I only need to acknowledge that when people act in spiteful ways, the reason is the same: lack of love, safety and affection in their recent or distant past. Hurtful behavior is a desperate cry for love that has derailed. Appreciating this helps me release blame and grudges. I direct my energy toward more effectively protecting myself from potential harm, instead of wasting it on resentful feelings. When I have taken good care of myself, it is easier to forgive because I am no longer under threat. At a safe distance, I am more generous and compassionate. Granting forgiveness, I cease being concerned about how others behave and focus on making myself stronger, healthier and happier. Forgiveness involves finding a takeaway from a hurtful experience; acknowledging that some sort of benefit has come out of it.

Forgiving is an act of generosity and kindness. What if the person who needs our forgiveness most is ourselves? Don't we have a responsibility to be tender and generous to our human, imperfect selves? Isn't *that* an act of kindness? I used to have a tough time forgiving myself. When judging myself, I was ruthless. I took no excuses and I made no allowances. I couldn't give myself the benefit of the doubt because I believed it wasn't valid.

I still remember incidents that happened many years ago. When I was a schoolgirl, many cats lived in and around our house. Every time a cat gave birth, my mom would let her and her little ones in the house to protect them from male cats who often kill kittens. When the kittens were a couple of months old, we would move them outside in the garden. One of our cats had recently given birth and we had her settled in the house with her babies. Their two-month anniversary was approaching, but my mom insisted that they needed a further couple of weeks in the house. It was a lovely Sunday morning in early spring. The weather was warm; the kittens were playful in their basket. My mother was away that day and as I set out for church, I thought it would be a pity to leave the cats locked inside on such a splendid day. I would only be gone for an hour. I would then put them back in the house. I let them out with their mother. An hour later, I came back to a massacre. What I saw on our patio haunted my dreams for a long time. I had made a wrong judgment, a terrible mistake. I had no excuse for myself. I should have known better. I should have listened to my mom; but I hadn't, and I couldn't undo the consequences. It took me years to overcome it and forgive myself, but I did.

If I can forgive myself, then forgiving anyone else is easy. I used to believe that I was a forgiving person, but I wasn't. Even though I reassured myself that I held no hard feelings, deep down not everything was fine. I wasn't pretending; I just couldn't realize the difference between rationally forgiving—in my mind—and emotionally forgiving—in my heart. I *wanted* to forgive, so I did what I thought I should. I suppressed my anger, disappointment and hurt so they wouldn't get in the way of me being a nice person. It was only when I let go of my own guilt that I fully released the blame I had been holding others accountable for. There was probably no noticeable change on the outside. The difference was in how I felt. I forgive myself not on the basis of excuses—I am not excusing myself—but based on the understanding that I am imperfect and I make mistakes.

Releasing a person through forgiveness gives me breathing space and freedom. I don't owe them and they don't owe me. Forgiveness is not only a gift for the person forgiven, but also a blessing to the one who forgives.

## Do-it-yourself or ask for help

I enjoy working on my personal development alone. It increases my self-awareness and improves my life experience. I take pride in being responsible for myself. Rather than waiting for someone else to fix my problems, I want to take ownership and control of my life. At times this can be difficult, and I then ask for support. Sometimes I just want confirmation that I am on the right track or to exchange experiences with a peer. It feels good to share. If things get tough or I want to embark on something new, I seek paid help. I want someone who knows more to show me the way, give me guidance and a push and get me started. There is nothing wrong with seeking help from peers or a professional. We think that the brave and strong don't ask for support. We tell ourselves, I shouldn't need any help; I should be able to handle this on my own.

I found admitting that I needed help hard when I was younger. I was raised to be independent and self-sufficient—an effective life tool—but occasionally asking for assistance is equally important. It is a brave step to make. Admitting my vulnerability and difficulty in handling everything by myself takes courage. Asking for help is an act of wisdom, self-love and self-awareness. At the end of the day, do I want to re-invent the wheel or buy four wheels and a chassis from someone who already knows how to make them? It is still me doing the work. It is me who is driving the car, steering my life. All I need is expert advice on which car to buy, or I may want counsel on which route to take from someone who has already been there. Paid assistance comes in various forms:

- Energy healers, who can perceive and point out underlying causes of health problems or life blocks

- Intuitive life coaches, who can help us train our intuition and improve our awareness

- Hypnosis practitioners, who can guide us on how to get in touch with our subconscious

- Psychiatrists, psychologists and other therapists, who can help us overcome past trauma and current drama

There is also an abundance of teachers and methods accessible over the internet. For me, the most important part is finding a teacher, coach, mentor, consultant or therapist that I am comfortable working with. They say that when the student is ready, the teacher shows up. Who is this teacher?

I am being taught, coached and mentored all the time. There are so many educators to choose from. I seek teachers, mentors, coaches and instructors who value and respect me. To be valued means that as a customer I am getting what I have paid for in terms of time, attention and content. Being respected means that teachers treat me as their equals. They don't look down on me or judge my choices. A judgmental teacher or a coach who tries to make me feel guilty, ashamed or fearful so as to establish a relationship of dependence accomplishes precisely the opposite. In my learning journey, I seek guidance from people who are content and peaceful in themselves. Passionate but not aggressive. I don't mind being challenged because for the most radical changes to occur a few buttons have to be pushed. However, I don't have to put up with coaches or mentors who unload their own insecurities on me.

Choosing a teacher is a decision to be made with the gut. I don't sign up for too much at once. I want to have some firsthand experience with the person before I invest more of my energy, time and money. I start by purchasing a simple and economical product to familiarize myself with the person and their work methods and check out our compatibility. I don't go for the mentor who guarantees making everything alright instantly by saying the magic word. I'd rather be guided to find my own way home. I want to acquire and practice new skills. This way, I learn continuously. Teaching students the art of learning is far more important than conveying specific knowledge. I am thankful for everything I have learned, but most of all I am grateful I have found people willing to share their skills with me. These teachers do more than serve me bread. They show me how to cultivate, harvest and bake. They are generous enough to support me in cocreating and upgrading. I respect that more than anything.

## Summary

- Healing comes in various forms. It requires self-reflection and willingness to let go.

- Surrendering to vulnerability heals our need to control every little detail, so that we can take control of living.

- In Experiment 7 we practice healing by releasing unwanted emotions and limiting beliefs.

- Our emotions are layered like an onion. Healing one layer, another is exposed and the process is repeated.

- We often inherit deeply rooted debilitating beliefs from our family. Healing them for ourselves, we are positively influencing our descendants' life experience as well.

- The technique of hypnosis enables us to directly communicate with the subconscious and expedite healing.

- We can find healing in liberating ourselves from limiting beliefs and fearful restrictive emotions.

- Forgiving ourselves and others sets us free and heals blame, shame and regret.

- The person best positioned to heal us is our self, but occasionally we may need assistance. It's important to select a coach or teacher who respects and values us.

# PART THREE
## RESTARTING

Part Three offers suggestions on how to be in charge, responsible and strong while, at the same time, true to oneself. There is immense power in being me. Instead of resisting life, leaking my energy here and there, I focus on being who I am naturally inclined to be. There is light, fire and passion in unfolding who I really am. There is joy and awe in self-discovery. There is unobstructed movement and unstoppable momentum in flowing with life.

Part Three is where I practice *being* instead of *doing*. By genuinely being me, I start regaining my power and re-establishing my place in the world. Even if it's just for fun, just for a while, as an experiment, it is worth giving it a shot.

# 24
# Re-establishing How Life Works

One of the first steps I can take to harmonize my life with what is natural is to keep myself grounded and present in my body. Grounding means being physically in touch with my surroundings, using my senses to experience the moment. Staying present in my body means that when things get tough and heavy emotions overwhelm me, I don't rush to dismiss and avoid them, trying to distance myself from the threat—the sensation in my body. I listen to what my body needs, accept my feelings, decode them and consciously seek to heal their root cause(s).

Another step I can take is making a habit of using my gut. The enteric nervous system, our gut, contains an extended network of neurons. It is a center of intelligence often called the "second brain," because it contains neurotransmitters that convey information to the brain in our heads.[70] As information is received *first* by the gut and *then* by the mind, a gut sensation is faster and less biased than a thought. We can distinguish gut feelings from processed thoughts, because gut feelings arise from the senses instead of being developed in the head—they show up as intuition.

A third step is aligning myself with universal natural principles, such as the law of attraction, the giving and receiving mechanism and the art of manifesting. My life unfolds more effortlessly when I play along with these principles rather than against them.

## The law of attraction

Two of my friends live in New York City. They were both born and raised there. One of them is in love with her hometown. She enjoys every bit of it and she's been fortunate enough not to have witnessed the ugly face of the city during her forty years there. Her experience of New York mirrors her emotions toward it: she loves NYC, and the city loves her back.

Her brother's experience is different. Even though he's been living in New York for thirty-seven years, he is fearful of the city. He's been mugged twice and was once caught in a crossfire. On several occasions he has witnessed crime and violence. He seems to attract the unpleasant side of the Big Apple. Is his fear a result of his experiences or are his experiences a result of his fear? It is probably both.

When I emit low frequencies, I get back more low energy. When I radiate in the high-frequency range, I receive more of the same. Perhaps not immediately, but eventually. Kindness and generosity may not always be reciprocated one-to-one, but they don't get lost. One way or another, they come back to me. Hence, the law of attraction.[71] What goes around, comes around.

When I give love, I receive love. When I send out fear, I get into a loop of attracting fearful experiences. My best shot for improving my life experience is to intentionally break this pattern and escape the loop. This intelligent energy exchange mechanism cannot be deceived by hidden agendas. When I fake kindness, this is precisely what I am going to get back: fake positive energy. If my only motive for being nice is to receive something beneficial in return, then what I receive is calculated, low-quality goodness. To obtain the best, I should also be willing to share my best.

When something seriously bothers me, I focus on a couple of good things and the situation gets a little better. I am not pretending to be happy when I'm not; I am deliberately finding reasons to feel better. Experiencing awe has a great boosting effect. It helps me expand, be happier and stronger. Problems seem smaller and more manageable, creating a ripple effect of high vibrations that attract more positivity. Bad things happen all the time. If I become absorbed by them, they get the better of me and I feel miserable. Misery attracts more misery, so more negative things show up. This goes on until I decide I have had enough and I resolve to break the pattern. The sooner I get out of this vicious circle of negativity, the better. I do this by reminding myself to celebrate my little victories, as trivial as they may seem. This gives me strength to decisively deal with the problem.

A London taxi driver once told me that the hardest part of his job was listening to his clients nagging all day, about pretty much everything. Externalizing my annoyance to a person who can fix a particular problem or to one who can offer emotional support is one thing. Complaining to someone who can do nothing about it and has their own worries is burdensome to them while not helping me. It can be satisfying in the short term, and I succumb to it, but when I grumble all the time, to anyone and no one in particular, it becomes a habit and I find more things to whine about.

Not complaining doesn't mean I don't face challenges. It means I don't feed the problem or allow it to grow, generalize and overwhelm me, and I don't dump it on others. Not complaining is not the same as suppressing my displeasure. It is choosing whom to complain to, when and how. It also means actively focusing my energy on solving a problem instead of leaking energy all over the place.

The ultimate application of the law of attraction is drawing abundance. To bring abundance to my life, I first create the feeling of abundance inside me.

I feel abundant when:

• I love my job and look forward to working

- I enjoy the time I spend with a person

- I settle down with a cup of coffee and my book

- I swim in the sea

- I hug my children

- I explore a city

It doesn't matter if I don't yet have everything I want or need. Abundance is not the sum of possessions, money or success. It is an energy. It is the feeling of being content, of always having enough of everything: health, love, success, wealth. It is the opposite of lack, scarcity, struggle or not being enough. It is cultivated inside and it then spreads outward. Being happy with what I have brings me more reasons to be happy.

## Giving and receiving

When I was little, I used to play a game with my friends. One of us held a small pebble in their palm and made a firm fist. The other kid's job was to take the pebble. Clenching our fists until the nails cut into the flesh, we were trying not to let go.

When I am emotionally or materially stingy, I feel my heart becoming smaller and tighter. It shrinks. Unwilling to give away belongings, love, compassion or forgiveness, I clench what is mine: my stuff, my pride, my ego, my dignity. I don't want to give, so I shut down my giving mechanisms. I close my palms, arms and heart tightly. My body enters a defense mode. In doing so, I also cannot receive. While my hands are busy protecting my own, I cannot accept a gift being offered to me. I am not prepared for any exchange.

When I give, I receive thankfulness and gratitude, and I set myself up for receiving. Energy flows from high pressure to low. To draw flow toward me, I create low pressure around me. I do this by giving. Giving away possessions, compassion and love, I create space for more of these to come to me. As I am prepared to let go, I loosen my grip. This reduces pressure in my body. Relaxing my muscles and opening my heart, I become more vulnerable but also more receptive. Good stuff flows my way.

In many meditation practices, palms are open, facing upward, and fingers are loose.[72] This posture enables giving, receiving, letting go and being open to the influx of love, grace and wisdom. Giving and receiving are not opposites. They are complementary. They result from the same mechanism. When I eagerly give, I effortlessly receive.

When I wish or pray for *something*, I summon energy toward a specific goal. When I pray for *someone*, I direct healing, supportive energy toward them. Praying for another person, sending blessings or wishing them well is voluntary. I do it because I want to, not because I have to. Often the beneficiary is unaware of this. After praying for a friend, I don't go back to collect debts: "Hey John! I prayed for you when you were ill last year. I now want you to lend me some money. You owe me!"

Caring energy can also take the form of practical action. An act of kindness is a physical manifestation of loving energy extending from one person to another. Helping someone and then seeking direct reciprocation is like cashing in a prayer or a good wish. This would demote my relationships to calculated transactions. It would mean that my strongest motive in helping someone is that they help me back.

As individuals, we are elements of a vast system: our Universe. In such a large system, reciprocity can unfold at a huge scale, if we allow it. When I help a person who is another element of the same system, I am actively contributing to this system. I am activating my account to give and receive. I can then receive support from the entire system through any person or any other modality. This is a compelling way of living. An individual directly returning a favor can do limited things for me, but the possibilities to receive support from the Universe are endless. I receive information, good luck, favorable conditions, gifts and surprises at times and from sources I least expect. This is the most powerful kind of reciprocity.

Paying kindness *forward* instead of back is the best way for big things to happen. It is difficult for two people to scratch each other's backs at the same time. A group of people standing in a circle can scratch one another's backs efficiently and effectively.

# The subtle art of manifesting

Manifesting is the art of creating the reality we want. This may concern an important aspect of life, such as health, family happiness and professional success, or it may be as trivial as finding a parking spot at the mall. It involves asking the Universe, God or my higher self to give me what I want. Asking means *making clear* what I wish for. It requires sending out a strong and targeted request about what I want to receive. To manifest, I create in advance the feeling I am aiming at once my goal has been accomplished. I magnify it as much as I can. I focus on what I want; nothing else. This puts me in the mood and mindset of a winner before attempting to materialize my goal. As a result, everything becomes easier and more enjoyable. I then focus my intention on the goal.

My manifestation abilities depend on intention and expansion.

## Intention

Intention means purpose. Do I know what I want? Am I clear about it? We often fall into the trap of directing our attention to what we *don't* want to happen. Manifestation doesn't work like that because it follows the law of attraction. Concentrating on what I fear might happen and trying to avoid it is more likely to bring me face to face with the result I dread. Likewise, pushing the unwanted outcome away usually creates a reaction and I may end up stuck with the undesirable version of the story. To manifest, I concentrate on the desirable end result. I make sure my energy is free from fear and other negative emotions such as revenge, bitterness, unworthiness, struggle, self-doubt. Such energies would attract more of the same. Manifesting is about *pulling* instead of *pushing*. I pull what I want to happen into my gravitational field, allowing it to gently fall into place.

Intention means focus. When I want a little bit of everything, my energy is fragmented. It is directed toward various goals and its intensity is divided by the number of different end results I am pursuing. Concentrating on one thing at a time increases the potency of my request and my ability to receive. I use affirmations and visualization to focus my energy on what I wish for. I channel my energy toward materializing it.

Intention means motive. My manifestation powers and my ability to expand depend on how I intend to use my manifestations. Manifesting involves power we may not be ready to handle. Substantial power in immature hands is a recipe for disaster. Universal laws of self-protection and self-preservation don't allow that to happen. The only way to access this immense creative power is to become a safe user. Safe users are those who are motivated by love. To unlock my manifesting abilities, I need to clear away fear and low emotions that may be destructive to others and myself. I then concentrate on the most desirable outcome.

## Expansion

I imagine this most favorable scenario in the greatest possible detail. I breathe in confidence and success. I magnify the emotions of satisfaction, contentment and joy, allowing them to expand and reach every cell of my body. I feel as though I have already made it. Even if I don't excel, this technique helps me do well enough. I expand by perceiving myself as an energetic component of the Universe. I close my eyes and mentally take myself 13.8 billion years back to the time and place of the Big Bang, the birth of our Universe. I visualize that point in space, which contains all available energy. I plug into the potency of this concentrated energy to power my manifestation. I visualize myself expanding from the heart, growing energetically larger than my physical body, occupying more space. I let go of fear, guilt, shame and blame, as these emotions keep me small and contracted. Being more spacious and impactful, I embrace everything with love. How can I expect the Universe to love me unless I love the Universe? How can I create anything at all without synchronizing with the Universe's creative energy? As a creator being, I can then proceed toward my goal.

Sometimes I fiercely want something, but I am blocking my own way to receiving it through self-sabotage. I have the intention, but my request doesn't go through. It hits the wall of self-limitation, scarcity, unworthiness and fear. Unconsciously, I may be unable to accept the good stuff coming my way because I feel unworthy, I pity or I punish myself. I may be unwilling to receive due to arrogance, excessive pride or a sense of superiority. At other times, I think I know what I want, but this is not what I need. This sends confusing messages to the Universe regarding what is best for me. I want to release these obstructing energies from my receiving channel.

When my manifestation attempts don't seem to be working, I doubt my abilities. Weeks, months or years later, it turns out the result was for the best. When I was in my twenties, I applied for what I thought was my dream job. I wasn't hired. A few years later, that particular company was implicated in a financial scandal and was dissolved overnight. Many employees got into trouble. By not facilitating me getting that job, the Universe had protected me. I was spared the loss of a job, being associated with the scandal or unknowingly being part of it, and the daily exposure to what proved to be a toxic work environment. Nobody likes failing, but sometimes small failures protect us from bigger disasters. The non-manifesting mechanism knows better. I remind myself not to be too disappointed when I don't get what I want. It may be for the best.

## Be careful what you wish for

When manifesting something using low-frequency energy, it generally doesn't end well. When I was at school, a friend of mine played basketball for the school team. He usually played as a shooting guard, but that particular year he was the coach's third choice and hadn't played much. He confided in me that sometimes he secretly wished something would happen to one of the other two boys so that he would get his chance to play before the championship was over. That evening, to our terror, shooting guard number two missed his footing and fell heavily on his hip. He was out for the rest of the season. My friend was summoned to play, but he was mortified. He didn't play well and confirmed to his coach that he was no better than option three. My Hindu and Buddhist friends would say he was punished by karma. I think more along the lines of the principle of cause and effect. He did something he regretted. His own guilt and remorse ensured that he didn't seize the opportunity. Subconsciously—and perhaps a little consciously—he no longer *wanted* to benefit from the situation. That night, my friend and I promised each other that the next time we wanted someone out of the way, we would wish for them to win the lottery and take a long trip to Hawaii.

We are unconsciously manifesting our reality all the time. When I don't want to give that dreadful presentation and I end up in bed with the flu, these are my manifesting powers giving me a way out. Sometimes our manifesting abilities are so potent that extreme things happen without us consciously giving our consent. A couple of colleagues and I were traveling across continental Europe for work, and we hired a driver who was supposedly familiar with the local road network. As soon as we got into his car and on the motorway, we realized something was wrong. The man was not a competent driver. He was driving below the minimum speed limit, occupied the wrong lanes, kept switching from one lane to another for no apparent reason and often drove in the emergency lane. I instinctively checked my seat belt. I looked at my colleagues, wondering whether I was the only one feeling uneasy. They looked concerned too, but none of us said a word. I couldn't shake the thought that a crash was inevitable and we would probably die on that busy highway. I closed my eyes and thought of my girls. My youngest was only three years old.

We finally took a slip road to exit the highway for a refueling break. I kept thinking that our only chance of surviving was to prevent our crazy driver from taking us back on the highway after the break. I closed my eyes and wholeheartedly wished we crashed before we had the chance to get on the highway again. I didn't really want an accident to happen, but if it *were* to happen, the timing was perfect. A second later, the car in front of us stopped at a red light and we smashed into it. The cars were both ruined and we were all bruised, but I was relieved and grateful: we were all alive and in one piece.

My wish had come true. I was both scared and pleased with myself. I had manifested a car accident because I couldn't see another way out. I then thought how stupid I was. The accident could have turned out to be a lot more serious. Was it really wise of me to ask for that when I could have simply and firmly demanded to get out of the car? I promised myself not to allow my timidity to override my better judgment, instinct and intuition again. I also made a mental note to be mindful of what I wished for in the future. After dealing with the insurance companies and having a short rest, our driver suggested hiring another car to continue our ride together. My colleagues looked at each other, unsure of what to do, but I had had enough. Knowing there wouldn't be a second chance, I spoke up and demanded another driver.

## Goals that score

My ability to manifest depends on the type of goals I set.

**External goals**, such as securing a specific job or being in a relationship with a certain person, are **forced goals**. As such, they are more difficult to manifest. I may have to go against another person's will to make them happen. This is energy consuming because I lose energy trying to overcome another person's resistance. Even if achieved, forced goals are founded on unstable ground. They usually result in temporary, short-lived satisfaction because they fulfill my superficial social needs.

**Specific, narrow goals** often prevent greater manifestations from happening. If I focus on a particular job, I may be blocking the way for an even better one showing up. Channeling my energy toward a more general goal, such as a job that makes me happy, works better.

**Internal goals**, such as being healthy, happy and fulfilled, are gratifying. Their effects are long-lasting because they satisfy deep personal needs. They are also easier to manifest. Whereas I cannot force a particular person to hire me, I *can* attract a job that is a good fit for me. This is a more **open-ended goal**, and I can make it happen without fighting against something or someone.

**Win-win goals** are easier to manifest. When I direct my energy toward someone else's benefit, it combines with their energy and creates a more effective outcome. When my intention directly conflicts with someone else's, whoever wants it more wins. Driving my daughter home from school one day, I was experimenting with my manifesting abilities. I asked for all traffic lights to be green for me to cross with no waiting time. It was all going well until the last junction, where the red light caught us. I spontaneously commented that my manifestation hadn't worked. My daughter unexpectedly apologized: "I'm sorry, Mommy. It's my fault. I was manifesting for a red light so we could listen to this song on the radio together before we reach home."

## Summary

- I can have a different life experience when I keep myself present and grounded, connect with my gut and align with fundamental principles of nature.

- According to the law of attraction, the energy I give away is matched by the energy I receive.

- Giving and receiving are complementary actions.

- Manifesting is the art of creating the reality we want.

- We sometimes manifest our subconscious wishes without being consciously aware of them.

- It's easier to manifest internal, open-ended, win-win goals instead of external, specific and forced ones.

# 25
# Being Me

Printers include the option "shrink text to fit." Its purpose is to fit a text larger than a page onto one sheet of paper by reducing font size and shrinking margins. It's handy and I have used it a lot. Years after I first encountered this function, it occurred to me that I was also applying this in life. I was often shrinking to fit other people's expectations and preferences, as well as social norms. How could I expect myself to expand when I was deliberately shrinking myself to fit in the tight frames of people's minds and expectations?

I want to feel free to be me, to dare to be different, without seeking approval or attention; to feel complete, safe and secure; to be enough. Being me might mean I seem "weird" to some people, but I can live with that. I don't care much about what other people think of me, not because I don't care about them, but because it doesn't matter. What matters is what *I* think of myself. Am I happy? Do I express myself freely? Am I responsible for myself? Does it feel like me? Who I am is not simple to define. I keep changing all the time. Seemingly contradictory aspects of me occasionally show up. When I clear away a behavioral pattern, new parts of myself are revealed.

I don't always manage to be consistent. I want to laugh in the face of adversity, but sometimes I get stressed and lose my composure. I want to be gentle, forgiving and peaceful, but I occasionally lose my temper. I wish I could perceive more and worry less, but there are times when I can't see beyond my nose and I worry about something trivial. I long for peace and tranquility, but now and then I find myself in turmoil. I love simplicity, but I often make my life complicated for no good reason.

This is fine. I won't always be perfect. I just need to be me.

## Know thyself

More than 2,500 years ago, in the Temple of Apollo at Delphi, Greece, priestess Pythia was giving her legendary controversial oracles.[73] These oracles could be interpreted in two ways and have two opposite meanings depending on how they were read. For example, when asked whether to engage in war, the priestess would thoughtfully reply: "War no peace." This could either mean: "War, no peace" or "War no, peace."

What is the use of such advice? Although the oracles may seem ineffectual, people were content to receive them and the prophecies made sense to them. They highly valued both the temple and the priestess.

Was Pythia an impostor? Was fortune telling at Delphi a scam?

Perhaps the value of these ambiguous oracles was that the receivers could interpret them according to their level of maturity and depending on their deepest desires, greatest fears, biggest regrets and self-doubts. Their interpretation was a projection of *their* world theory. Pythia wasn't leading people toward a predetermined result. That would impair their freedom. Instead, she guided them deeper into themselves, into self-knowledge and self-reflection. She offered them the confidence to make the choices they already wanted or believed to be best. Whenever I make a choice, I have no way of knowing how it would have played out had I chosen differently. Inscribed in the Temple of Apollo, the famous Delphic maxim "Know thyself" has been interpreted as "Know your limitations." Is this interpretation the only possible one? Perhaps we have been reading the maxim the way we *permit* ourselves to read it, when it could mean something different. It may serve as a prompt for us to search deeper and find the underlying emotions, the root causes driving our behavior and shaping our lives. It may be an encouragement for us to get to know our deepest desires, face our worst fears, clear them away and wake up to our true selves. It could be a calling for us to acknowledge our greatness, our divinity, our power, all we can be and all we can create, ultimately recognizing our incredible manifesting abilities.

## Nothing (in) excess

"Know thyself" was accompanied by another inscription: "Nothing in excess." We have interpreted this to mean "Do not exaggerate." This caption is attributed to Chilon of Sparta, one of the Seven Sages of ancient Greece.[74] Spartans were known for their minimalistic lifestyle. It therefore makes sense that Chilon's message advises "Refrain from exaggerations." Spartans were also renowned for their valiance and strength in combat. They won epic battles even when all odds were against them. In this light, Chilon's phrase could also mean "Everything is possible, nothing is an exaggeration," which is quite the opposite.

For over two thousand years, "Know thyself" and "Nothing in excess" have meant: "Stay average and mediocre. Do not excel. Remain ordinary. Don't go after the extraordinary." Re-interpreted and reread, the maxims could mean that nothing is far-fetched once we get in touch with our real selves and our true potential. They encourage us to search inside, find who we are and what we can make happen. Yes, I want to be grounded and aware of how far I can reach at any moment. At the same time, I want to keep searching deeper to find more of myself and my boundless potential. There is no limit to what we can accomplish. It is just revealed in batches.

## EXPERIMENT 8: CONSCIOUS BODY EXPANSION

The following two steps will help you release physical tightness and the associated emotional overload, and gather courage and determination.

First, deliberately relax your body. Starting from the toes and working your way up to the crown, identify areas of your body that feel stressed. Loosen the muscles by moving them a little. Unclench your fists and wiggle your fingers and toes. Let them take a natural, comfortable position. A loose smile, lips slightly apart, helps relax the jaw, the gums, the lips and the eyes. Allow the muscles in your legs, feet, arms and hands to relax by letting them drop and transfer their weight elsewhere: to the desk, the chair, the bed or the floor.

Second, consciously expand. Put both feet flat on the ground or any other surface, grounding yourself. Connect to the Planet and draw strength and confidence. Stand your ground and declare your right to be here. Slowly stretch as though you have just woken up. Breathe deeply and fill your lungs with air. Allow your eardrums to stretch. Observe how the flow of oxygen to the brain increases, boosting cognitive functions and lifting your mood.[75] Extend your limbs away from the torso. This releases tension and relieves muscle soreness and pain.

Practicing conscious body expansion often, I am teaching the muscles to seek stress-free positions as a self-relief mechanism, reducing chronic muscle tension.[76] It improves the natural posture of the body, but most importantly, it increases the feeling of safety and confidence, and it adds to my overall wellbeing. By expanding, I am claiming my space.

# The autopilot or me?

Another anecdote:

A new commander was appointed at a military camp. One of his first tasks was to inspect the camp. Two soldiers were guarding a bench at the center of the camp. The commander wondered why. He asked them, but they had no idea.

"We were ordered to guard the bench, sir," was all the information they could offer.

Curious, the commander phoned his predecessor to ask why it was necessary to guard the bench.

"I don't know," he replied indifferently. "When I took over, the previous commander had two soldiers guarding the bench and I just continued it."

The new commander got in touch with the woman who commanded the place ten years back.

"I have no idea." She shrugged her shoulders. "Two soldiers had been guarding that bench before I took command and I assumed there was a reason. You need to ask old Daniel. He was in charge before me."

The new commander arranged to meet retired old Daniel.

"There are always two soldiers guarding the bench at the camp's square, but I don't know why," he said.

The old man looked at him surprised.

"Soldiers guarding the bench? Hasn't the paint dried yet?"[77]

Many years ago, I visited an energy healer. I had intense and persistent pain in my body and no doctor had been able to find the cause.

"Your body is complaining because you are not being you," she said. "You have been operating on autopilot for so long that you can't even recognize it. Get out of the autopilot and you will be alright."

"What the heck is an autopilot and how am I supposed to get out of it if I don't know how I got into it in the first place?"

The good lady explained that we often force ourselves to do things we don't want to do and behave in ways that don't really express us. We become engaged with too many obligations without time to enjoy, relax and express ourselves. If this continues for a long time, we become accustomed to operating this way. We gradually forget that having a good time is a legitimate part of living. We underestimate the importance of self-expression, which is probably the reason we are here, on Earth, in the first place. Day in, day out, we do what we *must* and we rarely question any of it.

This is the autopilot: when I keep doing things without knowing why or when I can't perceive any value in what I am doing. It is the opposite of living intentionally and making conscious choices.

When on autopilot, I tend to react to what is happening around me instead of consciously responding or proactively making things happen for myself.

I become irritated, impatient or hostile. I am not being mindful of what I am doing, like my cat Boris when he wants to get out of the kitchen door and repeatedly bangs his head on the glass pane, each time hoping for a different result. Instead of purposefully steering the wheel, I allow habitual reactions to navigate my life. While on autopilot, I suppress my emotions because I either don't *want* to handle them or I don't think I *can*. My body becomes reactive. It uses pain to respond to the stress it is going through, trying to get my attention.

Once out of the autopilot, I am myself more often; I spend less time in worry-land; I am present and conscious in the moment; I make my mistakes—not someone else's.

So who is it going to be? The autopilot or me?

---

**EXPERIMENT 9: NEW ME**

**Design**

Take a photo of yourself at your best. Dress up in your favorite clothes, have a haircut or make some other change in your appearance. You may choose to do something silly or funny and pose at a setting that appeals to you. You want the new you to radiate through this photo. How do you beam? What is your frequency? What energy do you leave in your wake? Love, peace, joy, trust, happiness?

On the back of the photo, list your new self's five most important traits. You may already possess them or perhaps you are working toward them. These could be: health, enthusiasm, kindness, intelligence, sophistication, strength, creativity, perseverance, wit, spirituality...

You may also pick a role model: a fictitious person, a cartoon or an animal. Don't choose a real person: you are unique! Cartoons are fun and have superpowers. Wild animals are powerful, sensitive, intuitive and genuine. Find a beautiful or fun picture of your role model. List three superpowers you admire most in this character, cartoon or animal: acute awareness, crystal-clear clarity, increased agility, impressive adaptability, unbending resilience, outstanding courage...

This can be a short-and-sweet, half-an-hour fun project during a break at work, or an elaborate weekend-long activity. It doesn't need to be perfect. Don't overthink it or drag it out too much. Keep it spontaneous, simple and entertaining.

## Implementation

Now it is time to cultivate or enhance your personal characteristics and superpowers. To do this, start acting and behaving like you already possess them. You are not pretending. You are mindfully filling the role until it becomes a habit. It won't work 24/7 but that doesn't matter. When you catch yourself deviating, do your best to realign. Practice will keep the dormant Super(wo)man—who is always inside you—awake and active for longer.

While practicing, as much as I can, I deliberately focus on whatever makes me happy. Feeling happy, I consciously raise my eigenfrequency, my natural vibrating frequency. My vibrating molecules oscillate a little faster, a notch closer to the creative speed of light that transcends space and time and makes everything possible. As I approach a state of *resonance* with the Universe, I am setting myself up for miracles.

---

# Summary

- Being me means not shrinking to fit someone else's imagination.

- "Know thyself" may be a prompt for us to search inside and discover our unlimited potential.

- "Nothing in excess" may signify that anything is possible.

- In Experiment 8 we practice relaxing the muscles and physically expanding the body.

- We are operating on autopilot mode when we don't perceive purpose or value to the things we do by habit.

- In Experiment 9 we design our new self and we act the role until it becomes a reality.

# 26

# Living Skills

Taking note of my sensations (what the body senses), my emotions (how the soul feels), my thoughts (what the mind thinks) and my experiences (how life plays out), I get better acquainted with myself. Embodying my new self, I start living mindfully, switching the autopilot off. I observe myself, the people and the environment around me and I make conscious choices about how I act, how I speak, what I say, what thoughts I entertain in my head, what emotions I hold in my body. This requires slowing down and being deliberate instead of reactive in whatever I do. It is the skill of *being*.

Mindfulness literally means keeping my mind full with the task I am doing. It is the opposite of mind-wandering. When I write on the computer, I only think about my text. When someone is talking to me, I am only listening. When walking, I mind the road and pay attention to the surroundings. It sounds simple. In practice, though, I get distracted all the time. As soon as I notice it, the best I can do is return to what I am doing.

Mindfulness means not underestimating the power of little things. As trivial as they may seem, they constitute my reality and determine the quality of my day and, ultimately, my life. I don't have to buy the product in the most appealing box or the service promoted by the most persuasive advertisement; I can choose to buy an eco-friendly detergent or support an organization offering sustainable services and products. I can choose to enter a kitchen that smells of cinnamon instead of stinking fries. My seemingly insignificant everyday choices build up a lifestyle I enjoy and make up a story I can be proud of; one that reflects who I want to be and what I want to give to the world. Mindfully paying attention to what I enjoy and what I don't, what brings me distress, what relaxes me and what makes me happy, I can make subtle changes to my routine. Bit by bit, I construct around me a microcosm based on the habits I want to have instead of habits I have learned or inherited.

Mindfulness extends to being aware of how my actions impact others. I am mindful that the rest of my family don't like me turning on the radio on a Sunday morning, so I keep the volume down. When I am home alone, however, I pump it up. I am mindful when I talk too much and the person listening grows tired or impatient. I can perhaps find someone else to share my excitement with.

I am mindful of when I am not being me: when I am pretending, caving in or pushing myself too hard. When I identify this, I can consciously make more balanced choices and find ways to reconcile what I want with what is required of me. I am aware of the difference between being accommodating and constantly compromising myself or my life.

Mindfulness requires that I don't rush through life. When I slow down, time slows down too. Each moment lasts longer because it creates a more lasting impression in my mind. It is not wasted. As much as I can, I go placidly and take my time to *be*.

## Minding my vocabulary

The words we speak matter.[78] The words we *think*, those we keep to ourselves, matter more:

- The kids are driving me up the wall.

- My boss is suffocating me.

- My relationship has drained me.

- Why am I suffering?

- What have I done to deserve this?

- This is so hard.

- I can't take it anymore.

And the most impactful two words, "I am":

- I am a loser.

- I am exhausted.

- I am sick of you.

- I am never going to make it.

Self-talk is powerful, especially when the words "I am" are involved. We identify with whatever we are telling ourselves. Negative self-talk conditions the subconscious in an internal state of struggle, desperation and defeat. It is a merciless self-brainwashing mechanism that works quietly and efficiently until it creates a reality. Then, all incapacitating words we tell ourselves become confirmed by facts, not because we have accurately predicted them, but because we have unconsciously materialized them.

We use words and phrases that we pick up from those around us: parents, teachers, colleagues, media people, celebrities. Using dramatic language is contagious, even trendy, but words and phrases bear their own frequencies and may affect our mood in the short term, or emotional state in the long term. "Time is money." "Bite the bullet." "No pain, no gain." They seem innocent, but used extensively and repetitively they can create a subconscious debilitating belief or fuel a hidden fear. To jokingly say "I'm cuffed" when committed in a relationship may be subconsciously carving the conviction that relationships are restrictive, prison-like situations. We all have phrases we

spontaneously use more frequently, our "darlings."
When I pay attention to mine I identify deeply hidden thought patterns. If they are disempowering or misleading, I can replace them with more empowering ones.

Restoring my audible and inaudible vocabulary to either positive or neutral statements makes a difference. Rephrasing is more than putting words in a sequence; it leads to reframing: thinking differently. When a destructive thought or statement pops into my head, I take note of any fears it may be carrying and I clear them. I then substitute it with a neutral or a supportive thought. In time, my mind gets used to the new vocabulary and uses it naturally and effortlessly.

Repetition is powerful. What I hear again and again shapes my way of thinking. For this reason, I consciously choose the songs on my playlist. Song lyrics tend to linger in my head for hours. I don't want suffering, betrayal, despair or fear playing in the back of my mind all day. I watch comedies as an antidote to a stressful day. A twenty-minute daily dose of laughter should be prescribed by doctors. I take it right before going to sleep. It's a great way to relax and lift the day's load.

## Affirmations

Positive affirmations are the inspiring and encouraging words we tell ourselves to boost our confidence and feel supported.[79] They are an excellent way of training the mind to seek the good in people, things and situations. Repeating affirmations randomly during the day uplifts my mood. Applying them under hypnosis has an even deeper and longer-lasting effect in reconditioning my brain. Using them *after* I have cleared disempowering beliefs or emotions is most effective.

Affirmations are positive statements articulated in the present tense. I use the present tense because I don't want to wait for the good stuff to happen in the distant future. I want it *now*. Patience is a virtue, but when it comes to feeling good, the sooner, the better. "I am" (happy, healthy, fulfilled) is stronger than "I will be." I use only constructive language because this is what I want my mind to remember and my subconscious to learn. Repeating what I don't want is not an effective way of avoiding it because I keep reminding myself of the unwanted outcome, regenerating the emotions that accompany it. In addition to words, visualization enhances the attraction of high vibrations and helps affirm my desired reality.

Occasionally, when things are particularly tough, using present tense and positive vocabulary feels silly. Who am I kidding? Especially if I am in pain, it seems ridiculous to repeat to myself that I am healthy and feel fantastic. When this happens, instead of an affirmation, I pose a question:

- What do I need to do to be healthy and feel good?

- What is required?

- What does it take?

- How can I shift this?

The affirmation has now turned into a constructive question that carries inspiration, attracts helpful answers and motivates action.

## Yes or no?

We say yes and no many times a day, but do we use them for the right reasons? Some of us have a preference for yes. We like experimenting and trying things out. We may also want to please people. (There's nothing inherently wrong with pleasing people, as long as it is balanced.) Others are biased toward no. They save themselves from burnout but may miss out on wonderful life opportunities.

Generally, the more I say yes, the more I get up from the couch and experience life. I open doors, try things out and explore the world. I discover my limits and I expand them. I create the conditions for receiving more yeses. Saying yes to people makes it more likely I will attract positive responses if I ask for help in the future.

Sometimes, however, I say more yeses than I would like to. I don't want to displease and so I overpromise. As much as saying yes makes me look and feel good in the short term, it is a long-term trap. If I keep saying yes when I don't want to, unpleasant things may start happening:

- I deprive myself of my own needs and wants. As a result, I may eventually burn out.

- I resent others for having so much control over me, stealing my time, energy and happiness. I feel cornered or victimized.

- I feel bitter because I am not standing my ground and I easily cave in. I lose confidence and self-respect.

If it's going to be a yes, it might as well be whole-hearted or not at all. I say yes when my heart goes to something, even if it doesn't make sense to anyone else. If it feels light, then it's right. My daughter likes to ask: "When was the last time you did something for the first time?" I love this question. It motivates me to say yes to life.

Saying no is something I learned in my early forties. It's healthy to have priorities and know where to draw the line when it comes to other people's requests. Saying no sometimes protects me from unwanted and overwhelming situations. It gives me breathing space.

When I was younger, I felt guilty saying no to another person's request, especially if it was a friend or a family member. When I did, I spent substantial energy and time trying to defend my choice to them. Afterward, I spent even more time and energy trying to justify it to myself. I now know that a no is a no, and I don't need to make excuses for it. I don't always have to explain myself.

On the other hand, saying no all the time is slamming the door to unique opportunities and experiences that may not appear again. When I say no, it may be fear talking: fear of taking action, changing, risking, failing. A no keeps me stagnant when a yes would set me in motion.

I say no when I really don't want to do something, when it's against my instincts or makes me resentful, when it's not me. I decline requests that feel heavy and suffocating and invitations to places I will have to drag myself to. I say no to crowd decisions and harmful habits. As members of a large group, it's easy to get carried away by momentum and act in ways that don't represent us. Later, we regret it. Being mindful and conscious of our actions and nonactions helps to draw the line.

When I am indecisive whether it's a yes or a no, I close my eyes, relax my body and think of the question I am facing. I think or say "yes." If it lights me up and feels exciting, if it warms and calms my heart, it is definitely a yes. If yes feels heavy, uneasy or unclear, I think or say "no." How does *this* feel? If no feels reassuring, then this is the best decision. Occasionally, I get confusing or blurred messages. I then know I am probably not being honest with myself and I should get rid of whatever is blocking me from making a clear-cut choice. Is it fear? Is it procrastination? Am I going out of my way to please someone?

Yes and no are not necessarily opposites. They can complement each other. A healthy no can make space for many priceless yeses.

## Informed decisions

When making a decision that carries significant risk, I want to ensure I am making a conscious choice. I consider the worst-case scenario but only for a moment: not fearfully, just informatively. The principle of cause and effect dictates that any course of action I take will have its effects: costs and benefits, known and unknown. I ask myself: "Is it worth it?" Sometimes the price is too high for me to take a risk. Sometimes the potential benefit is too significant to ignore.

When a choice is right for me, even if it goes wrong, I know it was worth trying. I won't regret it. If it comes to it, I will bear the consequences without complaining. I have made an informed decision. There is confidence and peace in knowing that I consciously do what I do. Once I decide, I stop thinking of the worst. I release the associated fear or doubt and I concentrate on the ideal outcome. I expand and I condition myself to receive the best.

Computer science capitalizes on binary logarithms to represent any piece of information, no matter how big or complex, with only two symbols: 0 and 1.[80] This is a clever system that enables us to store, retrieve and use tremendous amounts of information using a yes/no, on/off, go/no-go, 0/1 representation. I use it to make choices intuitively when I lack the data to make an informed decision. I call to mind or visualize each alternative, I relax and I trust my body to show me whether it feels safe and comfortable with it. It is either a go or a no-go.

# Flow

I am mindful of when I am flowing along with life and when I oppose its natural course. When in flow, life is easy, effortless, interesting and fun. I feel happy and energized. I am not always like that. Sometimes I resist life. I don't like where it is going and I fight back. This usually occurs when I am not centered enough to accept there is a reason for whatever is happening or not happening. I get impatient and want results on the spot. I forget that instead of forcing things to turn out favorably, I can find the reason they don't and clear it. I recognize my resisting self because I become tense and stressed. I'm struggling. Pushing the river exhausts me.

When engaged in an activity I love, I can do it better than anything else. Immersing myself in what I find inspiring and intriguing creates flow.[81] When in flow, time passes without me noticing. Nothing can distract me from what I'm doing. I don't get tired, hungry, thirsty, hot or cold. I lose track of place and time and feel as though I could keep doing this forever. Synchronicities emerge as everything seems to unfold favorably and effortlessly. I am happier and more likely to succeed, attract money, power and recognition as byproducts of my work.

While creating their most profound work, artists, composers, poets, inventors and athletes report being in a state of flow. People in deep prayer or meditation describe similar experiences. We are not often in a state of flow. Most of the time, we don't enjoy what we are doing so we don't allow our minds to completely fill with it. As a result, worries, obligations, chores and daily commitments invade the thought space and distract us. Worries and distractions impede flow, like boulders obstructing the free-flowing river.

Being in flow is intense. It means focusing all my processing abilities on one task. It is the opposite of multitasking. The nervous system is incapable of processing more than 110 bits of information per second. To comprehend a person talking to me, I need a processing capacity of about 60 bits per second. I require another 60 bits per second to understand a second person talking to me.[82] To understand both people talking to me at the same time, I would need to process about 120 bits per second, which I can't do. When in flow, I am directing my attention, intention and energy towards a specific target. I am using my full processing capacity of 110 bits per second (or close to that) on a task that can be completed using 60 bits per second. This has the potential to create extraordinary results.

## Minimalism

Minimalism is not about having little.[83] It is about having what I need. No more, no less. It means making efficient use of available resources without creating unnecessary waste. A minimalistic lifestyle has nothing to do with abstinence and deprivation. It means getting rid of what is in excess and becoming a burden while keeping what is meaningful and fulfilling.

When I dispose of what drags me down, I feel lighter, happier, more balanced and efficient. Minimalism and abundance can co-exist. Avoiding my tendency to overstock, I am releasing the fear of scarcity. I can then enjoy the blessing of receiving what I want the moment I need it. This way, I always feel abundant because I don't experience lack. I am an abundant minimalist.

Genuine minimalists are renowned not only for their simple way of living but also for their clarity in thinking. They don't overthink. They keep their thoughts straightforward. This enables them to accept life as it unfolds and to flow along without much resistance and suffering. Minimalists, simple thinkers and peaceful people can be happy more easily. They don't burn out their brains chewing over what has been said or done. They don't load themselves with heavy emotions: accusing, blaming, envying, conspiring. They are not depleted by fear, fatigue, unhappiness and anxiety. They forgive, let go and move on. They live less through the mind and more from the heart. Their spirit is poor in complexity and rich in kindness and love.

To think simply is not to avoid thinking or to consciously remain ignorant. It is making a choice to accept what is, decide what should stay and let the rest go. Overanalyzing leads to paralysis because we get caught up in thinking without taking practical steps to improve our situation.

Simplicity is a choice. When I choose to perceive people and situations in an uncomplicated manner—without fuss or drama—they become easier to deal with.

# Decluttering

Decluttering means removing unnecessary stuff from an overcrowded place.[84] Both the process and the result are beneficial, so I practice decluttering on four levels.

## Physical space decluttering

Decluttering a drawer, a room, the house or the office is a liberating, reviving process. To declutter my closet, I take everything out and pile it up. For each item, I ask: "Stay or go?" I trust the first answer that comes through and end up with two piles. I give "go" clothes away to find a new home and become useful to somebody else. Physical decluttering is liberating because I let go of stuff and my associated fear relating to scarcity. I don't want to keep things "just in case." I put back in the closet what I *enjoy* wearing, which also gives me breathing space. There is room in the closet (and in my life) for new entries if and when I invite them in. I don't rush to fill the closet again.

The content of my closet mirrors my overall mood and lifestyle. Often, my choice of clothes reflects my emotional state. When I set out to make major life changes, I start with my closet. External changes are easier to make and often create the momentum necessary for internal shifts. I make them first to give myself a push forward.

## Mental space decluttering

I clean my house at least once a week, but how often do I clear my mind of the junk it is carrying? We clean and tidy our physical space more often than we clean and tidy our minds. We forget that if we never declutter our mental space, it will become dirty and stuffy, as any space does. We can't see our mental filth piling up, but we can feel it in the form of dark, incapacitating thoughts, insecurities and disempowering beliefs. Thoughts get entangled and mixed up. A chaotic mind makes relaxing nearly impossible. Making space for new creative ideas becomes difficult. An overloaded mind is a burnout risk.

If a disturbing thought keeps bugging me, to rid myself of it, I need to either identify the problem causing it and fix it, or pin down the associated incapacitating belief and clear it. To declutter my mind, I do my best to get pending tasks done as soon as possible. Then I can forget about them. I also take notes. I note my chores and appointments, as well as my creative thoughts. I get the best ideas and most profound AHA!s when I least expect them. Unless I put them down on paper, I can't relax, sleep or concentrate elsewhere. I am either too excited or fearful of forgetting them. When I write them down, I no longer have to keep them in my head. Meditation helps, as I practice clearing my mind even for a few minutes.

## Social space decluttering

Social decluttering may sound antisocial, but it is an important self-care practice. I find some people's energy overwhelming. When exposed to it for too long, I get exhausted. To avoid feeling tired and irritated, I seek to protect myself. I limit my interactions with these people, but I am mindful of how I articulate this in my head. Instead of thinking: "Gina is tiring; I'd rather avoid her," I mentally say: "When talking to Gina for too long, I get tired. I'd better get smaller doses of her." It is not Gina who makes me tired. It is me who gets tired when I have too much of her. This way, I don't blame Gina for *my* sensitivities and I don't hold hard feelings against her.

Social decluttering means I don't overload my week with outings and meetings I'd rather avoid and I have more time for myself, my family and friends. It protects me from feeling spent. I rarely follow social media. When I do, I am conscious of the emotions induced in me while scrolling. Following posts of athletes, scientists, artists and writers can be fun, interesting and empowering, but if keeping up with certain people on the internet makes me feel my own life sucks, do I really want to be doing this? I ask myself: "What is so upsetting yet addictive in closely monitoring the lives of others? Is it the lack of excitement in my own life? Is it that they have made things happen while I haven't? Are they living my dream when I am not?" When I know what is going on with me, I can then improve my own life and mind my own business instead of comparing myself to others.

## Emotional space decluttering

A heavy and messy emotional state is not visible to others. We think we can conceal it from the world, so we often leave it as it is. However, it affects our perception, life experience and reality. It makes everything more complicated and challenging. It is also reflected in our behavior and daily conduct.

Emotional decluttering is my personal favorite. I occasionally book a slot in my schedule to declutter my low emotions and work out what makes me feel uneasy, unhappy, resentful or scared. I tackle one emotion at a time. Is this good for me or not? Do I want it to stay, or do I want it gone? I ask questions and take note of the uncensored answers. I then proceed to release them.

# Relating to others

I want my encounters to be happy and energizing for all parties. I want people to feel relaxed, supported, loved and empowered when spending time with me. I also want to feel good myself. For all of us to be happy, we need to find that golden median between accepting and respecting, without suppressing or pretending. Sometimes this looks impossible. There are too many parameters to reconcile, some of which seem conflicting. Fortunately, there is another way. In relationships, simplicity is key. When I remind myself that all we want from each other is love, relationships become straightforward and easier. Loving people, I respect them naturally and effortlessly. Tolerating their eccentricities can even be amusing. At the same time, self-love safeguards me from overwhelm and burnout.

I am mindful not to always treat people as I would like them to treat me. Not all people share my taste, preferences, interests and peculiarities. I like doing things unplanned, but my partner doesn't. If I treated him the way I would like to be treated, he probably wouldn't like it.

My mood and emotional state affect how I feel about a person. When I am disappointed or dissatisfied with my loved ones, I don't like doing things for them. When I feel good in a relationship, I enjoy taking care of them. It depends on whether I perceive value in spending time *for* them. When I don't feel like giving, backing off for a couple of hours instead of forcing myself helps me depressurize.

Every day, we get tired from work, errands and other obligations. We look forward to reaching home in the evening to rest, process whatever has happened during the day, clear the tension away and have a moment of silence. Often, the people we love most—our children, parents, mates, siblings, partners, grandparents and roommates—are there waiting for us. Sometimes they are equally exhausted, but sometimes they are excited and want to share their news, or they may need help with something. I don't want my loved ones to experience my tired, spent and fed-up self every day. Sometimes it is inevitable, but if all I have for them when I get home every evening are my leftovers, what is the point of having close and intimate relationships? If I constantly show up agitated or worn-out, how can I express my love and spend quality time with them?

Isn't it a paradox that years pass and the people we love most get to live with a mediocre version of ourselves? We reserve our best selves for a job we may not even like or a boss we despise, while our partner ends up consistently experiencing our depleted side and our children only get what is left of us in the evening. Valuing my family, close circle of friends and business associates means showing up in full and high spirits for them at least half the time, without overspending my energy. If I do that, they are more likely to be compassionate and supportive when I occasionally collapse on the couch.

I want to be helpful to my loved ones, but I don't want to be *only* a fallback to them. In my close and intimate relationships, I need to share the good and the bad times equally. Always being the problem-solver and seldom the fun-maker, I risk becoming tired and even resentful. Sharing the good times helps us all experience the beautiful side of life and feel gratitude. It prevents burnout. Spending fun, entertaining and nourishing time together, I add to their wellbeing and they add to mine. We build optimism and resilience. Together we make days *good days*, so that the bad days are fewer, rarer and less hurtful.

# Summary

- Living mindfully means focusing my energy on what I am doing instead of letting my mind wander aimlessly.

- Our choice of words, both in verbal speaking and in our self-talk, affect our emotional state and life experience.

- Using affirmations is a good way of conditioning the mind to think constructively.

- It is important to say yes or no for the right reasons.

- Making informed decisions and being aware of the possible consequences is empowering.

- When in a state of flow, we are deeply submerged in what we are doing and focus all our energy towards it. This can yield phenomenal results.

- Minimalism is the concept of using our available resources and our thinking efficiently and effectively.

- Decluttering is the decongestion of overcrowded places, and it can apply to physical, mental and emotional spaces as well as social engagements.

- In getting to know myself better, I can interact with others more easily and meaningfully.

# 27

# Keep going

Zooming in and out reminds me that everything is lasting *and* transient at the same time. Whatever I do is forever, in the sense that it leaves its mark in the Universe. It has permanently been done. At the same time, nothing is forever, because no matter how deep a scar is, it can be healed. This helps me realize that:

- A hard period in my life will eventually give way to a more comfortable one, as long as I am conscious and mindful.

- My tolerances increase as I progress, and the associated distress is reduced as I learn how to remove myself from unwanted circumstances.

- I won't always be in an "achieving mood," and it's ok to take a break to reboot and recharge from time to time.

- At any given moment, there is something that is more important than everything else, and this is where I want to focus.

## This, too, shall pass

When I played board games with my little ones, I occasionally won and they lost. I then observed their reactions. Sometimes they got upset and cried. Occasionally, they threw the board and pieces on the floor. Their emotions were intense, but I didn't worry. I knew better. Indeed, minutes later they were fine, as though nothing had happened, because really nothing had happened. When I am overwhelmed, I tell myself that if I knew better, I wouldn't worry so much because this, too, shall pass. I zoom out of my little self and my stress levels drop.

When a person avoids, annoys or hurts me, I know better than to directly jump into drama. If I have done something I regret, I apologize and make amends for it, when I can. If they perceive me as an annoyance or threat because of their preferences or insecurities, I let it rest. Perhaps they need a time-out from me, just as I may sometimes need a time-out from them. Maybe they are not in the mood for my energy; maybe they have other priorities. It is also possible that I tire them, push their buttons or they just don't enjoy my company anymore. It is their choice. I just leave them be. I don't have to like it, but I don't need to suffer over it.

## EXPERIMENT 10: TESTING

Our spontaneous reactions are indicators of how we are conditioned and can therefore serve as a calibration mechanism of our state of inner peace.

When somebody says something nasty to your face, test yourself by evaluating how you feel. Regardless of how you act on the outside, you are looking for the emotions triggered within. Do you feel upset? Do you want to tell them off?

The car behind you bumps into yours at the traffic lights. Do you get stiff? Defensive? How long does it take you to chill down?

A shop assistant is being rude. Are you taking it personally? Do you want to shout back in his face?

If an incident evokes no negative emotion, I call it a *zero-response incident*. Anything that induces heaviness or makes me reactive carries an emotional load that exceeds my threshold of peace. When this happens, I proceed with investigating and clearing. Sooner or later, a similar incident occurs. I am then in a position to reassess my reactions and emotions. It is wonderful that, in due course, what used to be a provocative incident leaves me unaffected.

Overall, if people around me are frustrated, hostile, loud and offensive, but I consistently and effortlessly keep my serenity, then I know I have made progress.

# Recharging

Time on Earth is perceived as both linear and circular. Every twenty-four hours we experience a day-and-night pattern as the Earth rotates about its axis. Months succeed one another as the Moon loops around the Earth every 27.3 days.[85] We count years as the Earth orbits the Sun every 365.2 days.[86] The four seasons are continuously repeated. The almond tree in my backyard is a living factory. Once a year, it produces nuts. The tree is active and productive from late winter, when it first blossoms, to early autumn when it is time to harvest. Its changes are visible: snow-white little flowers, green leaves, tender green fruit, hard brown nuts. From October to February, the tree looks dormant. Nothing seems to be happening, yet we don't consider chopping it down. The tree is recuperating. It is regaining its strength and preparing for another production cycle.

When I feel unproductive, I remind myself that I don't always have to be in action. It's natural to slow down for a while. Every living being needs time off to refill its batteries between periods of intense activity and I am no exception. Our mortal bodies cannot always keep up with our endless to-do lists and our momentum for action. It's OK to take time off to recover and regroup when something significant or intense has happened or when I have just had enough. It's fine to take it easy sometimes. There is beauty in occasionally putting things on hold, turning inward, having a rest and appreciating the little things like a cup of coffee, a long game of Scrabble or a weekend in pajamas. When I can't pull off the day's tasks, instead of getting frustrated, I allow myself to enjoy an afternoon off for no reason other than rebooting. It's not failure. It's just wintertime.

## The most important thing

The most important thing is to know what the most important thing is.

When I have a lot to do, I get overwhelmed and confused. It is difficult to prioritize a long list, but it is quite manageable to distinguish the one most important thing at any time. Knowing what the most important thing is, at any given moment, makes prioritization simple and keeps me out of trouble.

When I am driving and my phone beeps, I am inclined to check it. What if it is something urgent? Then I ask myself: "What is the most important thing? Checking the message or staying focused on the road?" The answer is easy: "My safety and the safety of the rest of the users of the road network is a lot more important than instantly checking my messages." I focus on driving and I check my messages as soon as I pull over.

## Summary

- When we feel challenged, it helps to remind ourselves that this, too, shall pass.

- With Experiment 10 we assess our levels of inner peace by observing our emotional reactions to what could be provocative incidents.

- It's helpful to appreciate that we sometimes need time to reboot and recharge.

- It's important to be able to discern what *the most important thing* is at any moment and stick to it.

# Epilogue

Each one of us is at a different stage of our evolutionary journey. When a critical mass of people reaches a certain turning point, we can say that as a human family we are leaving an era behind, entering a new one. Since the last quarter of the twentieth century, we have been living in the so-called Information Age.[87] Thanks to telecommunications, digital technology, computers and the internet, a vast amount of information is widely available to roughly 5 billion people.[88]

This is the time to share knowledge. Experience and wisdom have been available for thousands of years but were kept within small communities due to geographical isolation and communication restrictions. The ancient Egyptians, Persians, Arabs, Greeks, the archaic Chinese, the early Japanese, the first Hindus, the autochthonous shamans in North America, Aboriginal Australians and more all held sacred pieces of the human intelligence puzzle. Perhaps, for the first time in human history, we can now reconcentrate some of this dispersed knowledge.

As the first wave of internet frenzy is subsiding and global mobility is becoming a routine, we may have come to that point where the Information Age gives way to an *Awareness Age*; a time when unprecedentedly more people will broaden their perception, enhance their awareness and access bigger parts of the puzzle. This is bound to lift humanity to a higher level of collective consciousness and enhance our sense of oneness. Consciousness is the master key for us to unfold, expand and thrive.

## One last story: I'll change when everybody else does

Back in third grade, the teacher scolded me for talking to the kid next to me during class. My automatic response was: "But Miss, others do it too and you haven't said anything."

Hardly an excuse, but expected of an eight-year-old. I am no longer eight. I am responsible for my actions and nonactions, relative not to anyone else's but to who I want to be. I am also aware that each person bears a unique impact in the world and that together we make up the reality that humanity is experiencing today. Zooming out, our individual impact is small at the huge cosmic scale. Zooming in, the influence I have on a small number of people (my family, friends and community) is huge. It is no longer insignificant.

This is where my ICR—my individual cosmic responsibility—lies. I am free to choose my life path, but I cannot pretend that I leave no impression on the world. My overall cosmic footprint raises or lowers the vibrations of the Earth and the Universe. The question is: "What kind of impact do I want to have in the world?"

My impact is measured both in terms of quantity and quality. It ranges in breadth, from small to large, and in depth, from fearful to loving. What if I can elevate the world's vibrating frequency by a fraction of a hertz?

In 1890, French mathematician and engineer Henri Poincaré gave birth to the concept of chaos theory:[89]

- There is no randomness. Behind every occurrence there is a cause—no matter how imperceptible. There is also a pattern, even though its scale may be such that it is impossible for us to perceive.

- The line between stability and instability is so delicate that tiny changes can have gigantic effects.

Half a century later, mathematician and meteorologist Edward Norton Lorenz coined the term "butterfly effect" to suggest that the time of formation and the path of a tornado are influenced by disturbances as minor as those caused by a butterfly flapping its wings days before the tornado occurs, thousands of miles away.[90] If a distant butterfly has the ability to affect a tornado, how can I negate or overlook my contribution to the world?

The butterfly doesn't struggle to change the weather. She behaves naturally and everything else falls into place as a result. What if I, too, can positively affect the world, shedding no sweat? Just by being me. By trusting my boundless benevolence, building bridges, vibrating high, by holding space for change to happen, by emitting love. Love is contagious. Once a critical quantity is unleashed, there is no turning back. One person may be all it takes to tilt the scale.

What if this person is me, or you, or us?

# Notes

1  Aristotle, *Physics*, translated by RP Hardie and RK Gaye. Available at: www.documentacatholicaomnia. eu/03d/-384_-322,_Aristoteles,_02_Physics,_EN.pdf

2  A Grisak (February 20, 2023) "Star legends, lore, and names from Native Americans," *Farmers' Almanac*, www. farmersalmanac.com/native-american-names-stars, accessed March 2023

3  Smithsonian Ocean (no date) "Weight of the world," https://ocean.si.edu/ocean-life/reptiles/weight-world, accessed March 2023

4  Madeleine (November 26, 2019) "Atlas holding the world story," *Theoi Greek Mythology*, www.theoi.com/articles/atlas-holding-the-world-story, accessed March 2023

5  DLTK's Sites for Kids (1998–2022) *Chicken Little: The sky is falling*, www.dltk-teach.com/fairy-tales/chicken-little/story, accessed January 12, 2023

6  H Rosling, O Rosling and AR Rönnlund (2019) *Factfulness: Ten reasons we're wrong about the world and why things are better than you think*, New York: Flatiron Books

7  A Maslow (2011) *Hierarchy of Needs: A theory of human motivation*, Kindle edition: www.all-about-psychology.com

8  Britannica (November 21, 2022) "Ohm's law," www.britannica.com/science/Ohms-law, accessed January 12, 2023

9  Sky History (November 9, 2009) *Thomas Edison*, www.history.com/topics/inventions/thomas-edison, accessed January 12, 2023

10 National Park Service (April 14, 2015) *1903 – The First Flight*, www.nps.gov/wrbr/learn/historyculture/thefirstflight.htm, accessed January 12, 2023

11 J Smart (2015) *The Little Book of Clarity*, United Kingdom: Capstone

12 Britannica (February 14, 2018) "Iphigenia at Aulis," www.britannica.com/topic/Iphigenia-at-Aulis, accessed January 28, 2023

13 D Purves et al, eds. (2001) "The audible spectrum,". In: *Neuroscience*, 2nd edition, Sunderland (MA): Sinauer Associates, www.ncbi.nlm.nih.gov/books/NBK10924, accessed January 2023

14 Government of Canada (November 20, 2015) "The Electromagnetic Spectrum," www.nrcan.gc.ca/maps-tools-publications/satellite-imagery-air-photos/remote-sensing-tutorials/introduction/electromagnetic-spectrum/14623, accessed January 2023

15 Newswise (May 2, 2022) "Study explains why sense of touch varies among individuals," www.newswise.com/articles/study-explains-why-sense-of-touch-varies-among-individuals, accessed January 2023

16 Boston University (January 6, 2022) "Why do we all feel touch differently?" www.bu.edu/articles/2022/illuminating-the-sense-of-touch-new-neurobiology-research, accessed January 2023

17 S Moylan (May 16, 2015) "Enhancing the senses: Improve your sense of touch," News Corp Australia Network, www.news.com.au/lifestyle/health/enhancing-the-senses-improve-your-sense-of-touch/news-story/f5ff38173b5ec9de42fa2ca15ac3a905, accessed January 2023

18 Science Direct (2010) "Taste bud," www.sciencedirect.com/topics/immunology-and-microbiology/taste-bud, accessed January 2023

19 M Kronenbuerger and M Pilgramm (October 24, 2022) "Olfactory training," *StatPearls*, www.ncbi.nlm.nih.gov/books/NBK567741, accessed January 2023

20  H Riebeek (July 7, 2009) "Planetary motion: The history
    of an idea that launched the scientific revolution," NASA
    Earth Observatory, www.earthobservatory.nasa.gov/
    features/OrbitsHistory, accessed January 2023
21  Britannica (December 26, 2022) "Perception," www.
    britannica.com/topic/perception, accessed January 2023
22  J Smart (2015) *The Little Book of Clarity*, United Kingdom:
    Capstone
23  Aviation Intelligence Unit Portal (2023) "Flight information
    region," www.ansperformance.eu/acronym/fir, accessed
    January 2023
24  M Mowbray (no date) "Prefix 'Clair'," *Sixth Sense*, https://
    sixthsensereader.org/about-the-book/abcderium-index/
    clair-prefix-the, accessed January 2023
25  R Ross (April 26, 2017) "Eureka! The Archimedes
    Principle," *Live Science*, www.livescience.com/58839-
    archimedes-principle, accessed January 2023
26  *National Geographic* (1996–2023) "Isaac Newton: Who
    he was, why apples are falling," https://education.
    nationalgeographic.org/resource/isaac-newton-who-he-
    was-why-apples-are-falling, accessed January 2023
27  G Turner (Sep 13, 2020) "How Einstein's insight, the 'real
    valuable thing is intuition,' can help writers," The Writing
    Cooperative, https://writingcooperative.com/how-
    einsteins-insight-the-real-valuable-thing-is-intuition-can-
    help-writers-8cc4cd8db451, accessed January 2023
28  J Currivan (2017) *The Cosmic Hologram: In-formation at the
    center of creation*, Vermont: Inner Traditions
29  Ibid.
30  V Stein (February 1, 2022) "Einstein's theory of special
    relativity," *Space*, www.space.com/36273-theory-special-
    relativity, accessed January 2023
31  J Currivan (2017) *The Cosmic Hologram*
32  Ibid.
33  Britannica (September 6, 2022) "Planck's constant," www.
    britannica.com/science/Plancks-constant, accessed
    January 2023
34  YJ John (March 21, 2016) "The 'streetlight effect': A
    metaphor for knowledge and ignorance'," *3 Quarks
    Daily*, www.3quarksdaily.com/3quarksdaily/2016/03/
    the-streetlight-effect-a-metaphor-for-knowledge-and-
    ignorance, accessed January 2023

35  A Ranadive (June 1, 2017) "Einstein's way of thinking," *Medium*, https://medium.com/@ameet/einsteins-way-of-thinking-b1046a3f6bde, accessed January 2023

36  G Muccino, dir. (2006) The Pursuit of Happyness, Columbia Pictures

37  Matthew 14:28–31 (NIV)

38  Theoei (no date) "Khimaira," www.theoi.com/Ther/Khimaira.html, accessed March 2023

39  Science Direct (2017) "Pressure vessel codes," www.sciencedirect.com/topics/engineering/pressure-vessel-codes, accessed January 2023

40  Forever Conscious (2022) "6 signs that energy is being released from the body," www.foreverconscious.com/6-signs-energy-released-body, accessed January 2023

41  J Ramirez (2014) "The integrative role of the sigh in psychology, physiology, pathology, and neurobiology," *Progress in Brain Research*, 209 pp91–129, www.ncbi.nlm.nih.gov/pmc/articles/PMC4427060, accessed January 2023

42  L Newhouse (March 1, 2021) "Is crying good for you?" Harvard Health Publishing, www.health.harvard.edu/blog/is-crying-good-for-you-2021030122020, accessed January 2023

43  NHS (August 15, 2022) "Breathing exercises for stress," www.nhs.uk/mental-health/self-help/guides-tools-and-activities/breathing-exercises-for-stress, accessed January 2023

44  C Oestreicher (September 2007) "A history of chaos theory," *Dialogues in Clinical Neuroscience*, 9(3) pp279–89, https://ncbi.nlm.nih.gov/pmc/articles/PMC3202497, accessed January 2023

45  J Leonard (January 8, 2020) "Homer's hospitality: The ancient roots of Greek philoxenia," *Greece Is*, www.greece-is.com/homers-hospitality-the-ancient-roots-of-greek-philoxenia, accessed March 2023

46  L Rosenstiehl (June 30, 2022) "Liver: The source of emotions, according to ancient Greeks," *Greek Reporter*, www.greekreporter.com/2022/06/30/liver-the-source-of-emotions-according-to-ancient-greeks, accessed January 2023

47  D King (April 9, 2014) "Top 3 ways an activated thymus can change your life," www.healyourlife.com/top-3-ways-an-activated-thymus-can-change-your-life, accessed January 2023

48  Britannica (Aug 16, 2022) "E = mc2 equation," www.
    britannica.com/science/E-mc2-equation, accessed
    January 30, 2023

49  H McElhatton (Nov 4, 2019) "A beautiful world: Molecules,
    the architecture of everything," *MPR News*, www.mprnews.
    org/story/2019/11/04/a-beautiful-world-molecules-the-
    architecture-of-everything, accessed March 2023

50  Currivan (2017) *The Cosmic Hologram*

51  Britannica (September 6, 2022) "Planck's constant"

52  R Hawkins (2013) *Power vs. Force*, UK: Hay House Inc

53  J Orloff, MD (2017) *The Empath's Survival Guide: Life
    strategies for sensitive people*, Colorado: Sounds True Inc.

54  C Zimmer (October 23, 2013) "How many cells are in your
    body?" *National Geographic*, www.nationalgeographic.com/
    science/article/how-many-cells-are-in-your-body, accessed
    March 2023

55  SciTechDaily (September 2, 2022) "Single cells are more
    intelligent than scientists previously thought," www.
    scitechdaily.com/single-cells-are-more-intelligent-than-
    scientists-previously-thought, accessed January 2023

56  J Currivan (2017) *The Cosmic Hologram*

57  Ibid.

58  Ibid.

59  Energy Education (no date) "Size of the universe," www.
    energyeducation.ca/encyclopedia/Size_of_the_universe,
    accessed January 2023

60  J Currivan (2017) *The Cosmic Hologram*

61  Worldometer (2022) "Current World Population,"
    www.worldometers.info/world-population, accessed
    January 2023

62  B Brown (2012) *The Power of Vulnerability: Teachings of
    authenticity, connection, and courage*, Colorado: Sounds True
    Inc.

63  US Geological Survey (no date) "Ninety percent of an
    iceberg is below the waterline," Water Science School,
    www.usgs.gov/media/images/ninety-percent-iceberg-
    below-waterline, accessed January 2023

64  J Currivan (2017) *The Cosmic Hologram*

65  Science Direct (2013) "Brain waves," www.sciencedirect.
    com/topics/agricultural-and-biological-sciences/brain-
    waves, accessed March 2023

66  The Brain Wave Audio Expert (2010–2023) "What are
    epsilon and lambda waves?" www.binauralbeatsfreak.

com/brainwave-entrainment/epsilon-waves-lambda-waves, accessed January 2023

67  J Murdoch (July 15, 2020) "Humans have more than 6,000 thoughts per day, psychologists discover," *News Week*, www.newsweek.com/humans-6000-thoughts-every-day-1517963, accessed January 2023; Healthy Brains (2022) "You are your brain," Cleveland Clinic, www.healthybrains.org/brain-facts, accessed January 2023

68  M Peer (2023) *Perfect Weight Forever*, Kindle edition, www.perfectweightforever.com; M Peer (May 30, 2019) "6 facts about what sugar does to your body," www.marisapeer.com/what-does-sugar-do-to-your-body, accessed January 2023

69  DA Soskis, EC Orne, MT Orne and DF Dinges (1989) "Self-hypnosis and meditation for stress management: A brief communication," *International Journal of Clinical and Experimental Hypnosis*, 37:4, pp285–289, https://www.tandfonline.com/doi/abs/10.1080/00207148908414483, accessed March 2023

70  A Hadhazy (February 12, 2010) "Think twice: How the gut's 'second brain' influences mood and well-being," *Scientific American*, www.scientificamerican.com/article/gut-second-brain, accessed January 2023

71  StarChild (2001) "StarChild question of the month for February 2001," https://starchild.gsfc.nasa.gov/docs/StarChild/questions/question30.html, accessed January 2023

72  F Gonçalves Rocha (2020–2023) "The meditation posture: What is the best position for meditation?" Center for Human Flourishing, www.center-for-human-flourishing.org/beginners-guide/the-meditation-posture-what-is-the-best-position-for-meditation, accessed January 2023

73  A Tsaroucha (2012) "Temple of Apollo at Delphi," http://odysseus.culture.gr/h/2/eh251.jsp?obj_id=1318, accessed March 2023

74  RealGreekExperiences (January 5, 2023) "The Delphic maxims: Ancient Greek wisdom," https://realgreekexperiences.com/delphic-maxims, accessed March 2023

75  A Morland (January 10, 2020) "The benefits of oxygen," Valeo Health and Wellness Center, www.valeowc.com/the-benefits-of-oxygen, accessed January 2023

76  American Psychological Association (November 1, 2018) "Stress effects on the body," www.apa.org/topics/stress/body, accessed January 2023

77  iFunny (December 3, 2020) "This is how traditions are born," www.ifunny.co/picture/ss-this-is-how-anew-camp-commander-was-appointed-and-WjnDHMfB8, accessed January 2023

78  Psych Central (2005–2023) "How do words affect the brain?" www.psychcentral.com/blog/words-can-change-your-brain#effects-on-the-brain, accessed January 2023

79  CN Cascio et al (April 2016) "Self-affirmation activates brain systems associated with self-related processing and reward and is reinforced by future orientation," *Social Cognitive and Affective Neuroscience*, 11(4) pp621–9, https://pubmed.ncbi.nlm.nih.gov/26541373, accessed February 2023

80  Britannica (August 29, 2022) "Numerals and numeral systems," www.britannica.com/science/numeral/Development-of-modern-numerals-and-numeral-systems, accessed January 2023

81  M Csikszentmihalyi (2008) *Flow: The psychology of optimal experience*, New York: Harper Perennial

82  M Csikszentmihalyi (2004) "Flow, the secret to happiness," TED Talk, www.ted.com/talks/mihaly_csikszentmihalyi_flow_the_secret_to_happiness?language=en, accessed March 2023

83  I Garrido (2005–2023) "10 easy ways to start thinking as a minimalist," *LifeHack*, www.lifehack.org/419088/10-easy-ways-to-start-thinking-as-a-minimalist, accessed January 2023

84  A Beckwith and E Parkhurst (July 1, 2022) "The mental benefits of decluttering," https://extension.usu.edu/mentalhealth/articles/the-mental-benefits-of-decluttering, accessed January 2023

85  NASA Science, "What do you wonder?" https://moon.nasa.gov/inside-and-out/top-moon-questions, accessed January 2023

86  NASA (June 9, 2015) "Revolve," www.nasa.gov/audience/forstudents/k-4/dictionary/Revolve.html, accessed January 2023

87  Merriam Webster (no date) "Information age," https://www.merriam-webster.com/dictionary/Information%20Age, accessed January 2023

88  DataReportal (2023) "Digital around the world," https://datareportal.com/global-digital-overview, accessed March 2023

89  C Oestreicher (September 2007) "A history of chaos theory"

90  Ibid.

# Acknowledgments

First, I want to thank my personal development teachers. Without them, this book wouldn't have been possible and I wouldn't be who I am. I learned:

- Hypnosis from Marisa Peer

- Mind control from Laura Silva

- Faster Emotional Freedom Techniques (EFT) from Robert Smith

- Positive psychology from Dr. Barbara L. Fredrickson via Coursera

- The science of happiness through the University of California, Berkeley, via edX

- How to develop my intuition from Christie Sheldon

- How to meditate from Deborah King

- How to forgive and let go from Alan Cohen

I have also learned about:

- Vulnerability from Brené Brown[62]

- Flow from Michael Csikszentmihalyi[82,83]

- Empathy from Judith Orloff[53]

This book is an amalgam of what I have learned and experienced during my own self-discovery journey. I am grateful to my coaches and teachers, but they are not accountable for what I have distilled from their teachings.

I want to thank my partner, my daughters and my parents for their love and support. Thanks, Dad, for reading this three or four times. A big thanks to Kasha Shana, Lisa Bell, Lauren Nicole, Oriana Charalambidou, Andreas Messaritis and my friend Ling So for helping me get over some of my junk. Thank you so much, Kathy, for bearing with me. Thank you Anke, Sarah, Kinga, Lucy, Joe and the rest of the Rethink Press team. Tess, a special thanks to you for your patience during editing.

# The Author

Koralia was born in 1976 in Cyprus. She studied civil and environmental engineering at Imperial College London. For twenty years she worked as a management consultant. In 2019, she co-authored the book *Executive Excellence: Combine Leadership and Management to Create and Deliver Value*. She then enhanced her intuition and trained in hypnosis. She now offers intuitive coaching and personal development mentoring. She divides her time between Cyprus and Belgium.

🌐 www.koraliatimotheou.com

📘 www.facebook.com/profile.php?id=100015068409407

💼 www.linkedin.com/in/koralia-timotheou-7546021b

📷 @koraliatimotheou